W9-BBY-173

Silver Burdett Ginn
Mathematics

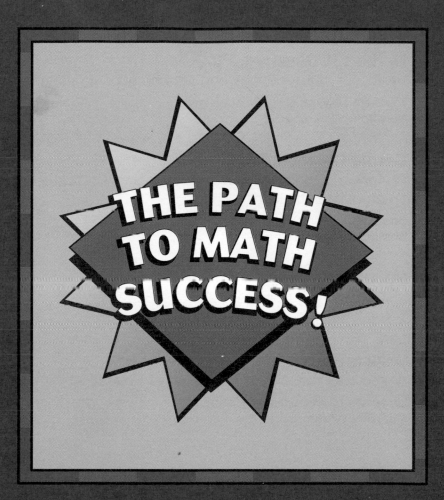

THE PATH
TO MATH
SUCCESS!

Silver Burdett Ginn

Parsippany, NJ

Atlanta, GA • Deerfield, IL • Irving, TX • Needham, MA • Upland, CA

Program Authors

Francis (Skip) Fennell, Ph.D.
Professor of Education and Chair, Education Department

Western Maryland College
Westminster, Maryland

Joan Ferrini-Mundy, Ph.D.
Professor of Mathematics

University of New Hampshire
Durham, New Hampshire

Herbert P. Ginsburg, Ph.D.
Professor of Psychology and Mathematics Education

Teachers College, Columbia University
New York, New York

Carole Greenes, Ed.D.
Professor of Mathematics Education and Associate Dean,
 School of Education

Boston University
Boston, Massachusetts

Stuart J. Murphy
Visual Learning Specialist

Evanston, Illinois

William Tate, Ph.D.
Associate Professor of Mathematics Education

University of Wisconsin-Madison
Madison, Wisconsin

Acknowledgments appear on page 388, which constitutes an extension of this copyright page.

©2001 Silver Burdett Ginn Inc. All rights reserved. Printed in the United States of America. This publication, or parts thereof, may not be reproduced in any form by photographic, electronic, mechanical, or any other method, for any use, including information storage and retrieval, without written permission from the publisher.

ISBN 0-382-34891-5

13 14 15 BAM 08 07 06 05

Silver Burdett Ginn
299 Jefferson Road, P.O. Box 480
Parsippany, NJ 07054-0480

Senior Author

Mary Cavanagh, M.S.
Principal Investigator, Math,
 Science, and Beyond

Solana Beach School District
Solana Beach, California

Grade Level Authors

Jennie Bennett, Ed.D.
Instructional Mathematics Supervisor

Houston Independent School District
Houston, Texas

Charles Calhoun, Ph.D.
Associate Professor of Elementary
 Education Mathematics

University of Alabama at Birmingham
Birmingham, Alabama

Lucille Croom, Ph.D.
Professor of Mathematics

Hunter College of the City University
 of New York
New York, New York

Robert A. Laing, Ph.D.
Professor of Mathematics Education

Western Michigan University
Kalamazoo, Michigan

Kay B. Sammons, M.S.
Supervisor of Elementary Mathematics

Howard County Public Schools
Ellicott City, Maryland

Marian Small, Ed.D.
Professor of Mathematics Education

University of New Brunswick
Fredericton, New Brunswick, Canada

Contributing Authors

Stephen Krulik, Ed.D.
Professor of Mathematics Education

Temple University
Philadelphia, Pennsylvania

Donna J. Long
Mathematics/Title 1 Coordinator

Metropolitan School District of
 Wayne Township
Indianapolis, Indiana

Jesse A. Rudnick, Ed.D.
Professor Emeritus of Mathematics
 Education

Temple University
Philadelphia, Pennsylvania

Clementine Sherman
Director, USI Math and Science

Dade County Public Schools
Miami, Florida

Bruce R. Vogeli, Ph.D.
Clifford Brewster Upton Professor
 of Mathematics

Teachers College, Columbia University
New York, New York

Contents

Chapter 1

Exploring Numbers and Patterns

Chapter Theme: Counting Carnival

Math Storybook: *Fun at the Fair*

Chapter 2

Understanding Addition

Chapter Theme: Creepy-Crawly Critters

Math Storybook: *The Bug Book*

Chapter 3

Understanding Subtraction

Chapter Theme: Kid's Play

Math Storybook: *Miss Terry's Toy Store*

Chapter 4

Introducing Basic-Fact Strategies

Chapter Theme: On the Move

Math Storybook: *Let's Go!*

Geometry and Fractions

Chapter Theme: Art Action

Math Storybook: *Stitching Stories*

---- *Chapter Resources* ----

Patterns and Numbers to 100

Chapter Theme: Home Zone

Math Storybook: *Too Many Birds!*

Money

Chapter Theme: What a Deal!

Math Storybook: *Silly Sam*

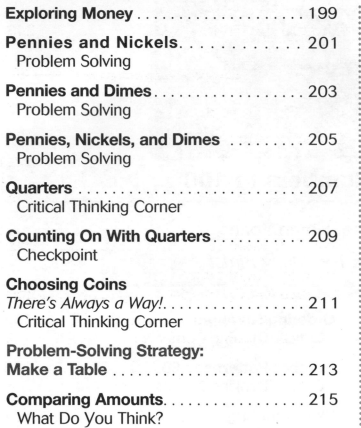

Relating Addition and Subtraction

Chapter Theme: Munch a Bunch

Math Storybook: *Behind the Door*

Time and Probability

Chapter Theme: All in a Day

Math Storybook: *A Rainy Day*

Chapter 10

Measurement

Chapter Theme: Silly Sizes

Math Storybook: *How Do You Measure a Pig?*

Hooray for you, Big Bert!

Chapter 11

Addition and Subtraction to 18

Chapter Theme: The Desert

Math Storybook: *Look Who's Here!*

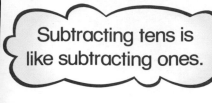
Subtracting tens is like subtracting ones.

Exploring Two-Digit Addition and Subtraction

Chapter Theme: In My Pocket

Math Storybook: *Po Lan's Pocket*

Fun at the Fair

written by Shereen Gertel Rutman

illustrated by Patrick Girouard

This Math Storybook

belongs to

Ashley

The Gladstone Geese are at the fair.
How many geese are there?
Count the geese.
Count each one.

© Silver Burdett Ginn Inc. All rights reserved.

The geese see horses at the fair.
How many horses are there?
Count the horses.
Count each one. 4

The geese see silly hats at the fair.
How many silly hats are there?
Count the silly hats.
Count each one.

© Silver Burdett Ginn Inc. All rights reserved

Count the things you see at the fair.
Groups of 1 to 12 will be there.

INTERNET ACTIVITY
www.sbgmath.com

A Note to the Family

**Here are some learning ideas
you can share with your child.**

Enjoy *Fun at the Fair* Together

- Read each page with your child. Then count some of the items on the page together.

- Help your child find all the groups on the last page of the story. Some possible groups in the picture are 1 ticket booth, 2 drinks with straws, 3 flowers, 4 carousel horses, 5 candy apples, 6 silly hats, 7 geese, 8 tickets for rides, 9 balloons, 10 blue balls, 11 bees, and 12 ice-cream cones.

At-Home Activity

- Use mealtime or cleanup time at home as a fun way to practice counting. Have your child help set the table. As she or he places each napkin down, count out loud. Encourage your child to count, too. Repeat this activity with the cutlery, glasses, and plates.

- Pick an item in the house that needs to be put away. For example, ask your child to put away 6 blocks. Then ask your child to put away 4 books. Repeat this activity, changing the number each time. You can take turns asking each other to clean up a certain number of objects. The room will be clean in a short time, and your child will have a great time playing the game!

Read More About It!

To read more about counting, look for these books in your local library.

- *Have You Seen My Duckling?* by Nancy Tafuri (Greenwillow, 1985)
- *One, Two, Three, Count With Me* by Catherine and Laurence Anholt (Viking, 1993)
- *Ten Black Dots* by Donald Crews (Greenwillow, 1986)

Visit Our Web Site!

INTERNET ACTIVITY
www.sbgmath.com

© Silver Burdett Ginn Inc. All rights reserved.

Name_____

Use . Then draw.

1. Draw a group with the **same** number.

   ● ●

2. Draw a group with **more**.

3. Draw a group with **fewer**.

Home Connection Show your child a group of household objects.
Ask him or her to show you either the same number, more, or fewer objects.

one   1

Look at each group.
Draw a group to show I fewer.
Draw a group to show I more.

1.

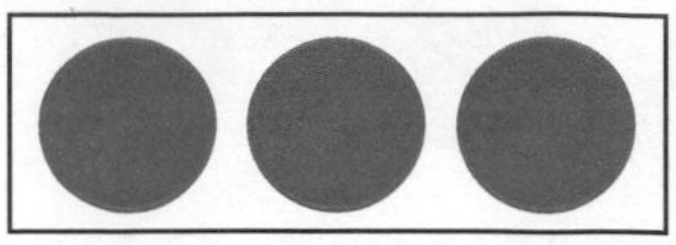

I fewer	I more

2.

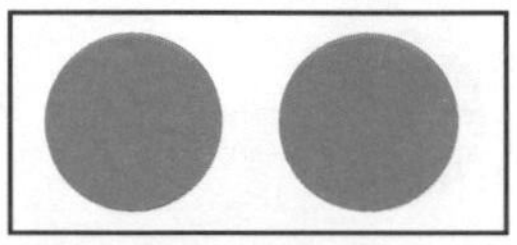

I fewer	I more

3.

I fewer	I more

Make Your Own

© Silver Burdett Ginn Inc. All rights reserved.

1
one

2
two

3
three

4
four

5
five

Use  to show each number.

Draw to show how many.

1. ⭕ ⭕ ⭕	2.
3	5
3.	**4.**
1	4
5.	**6.**
2	3

🏠 **Home Connection** Children need many opportunities to show numbers. Ask your child to say a number and hold up that many fingers.

three   **3**

Circle the groups that show each number.

1.

3
three

2.

1
one

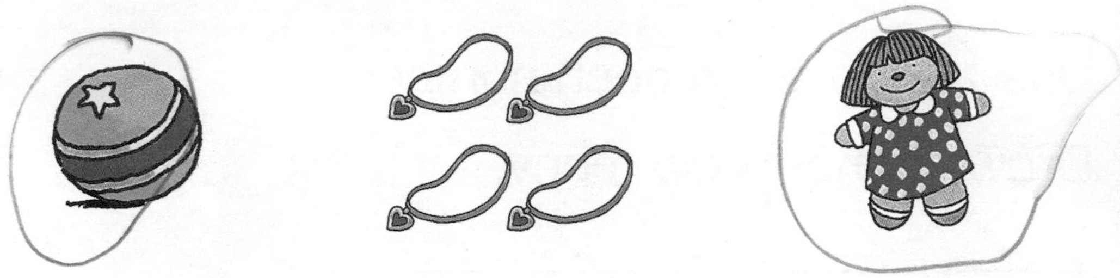

3.

4
four

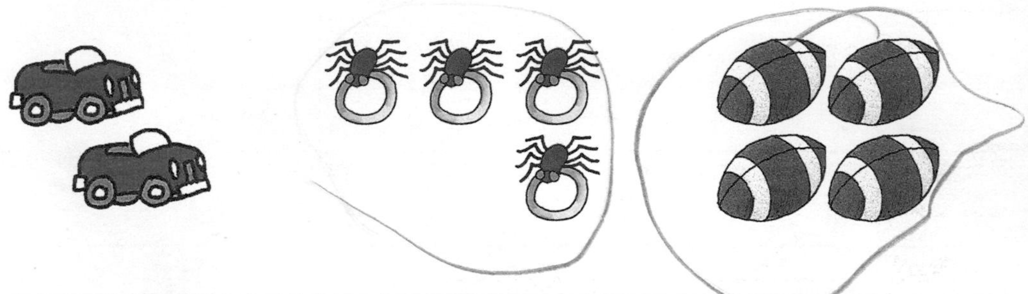

4.

2
two

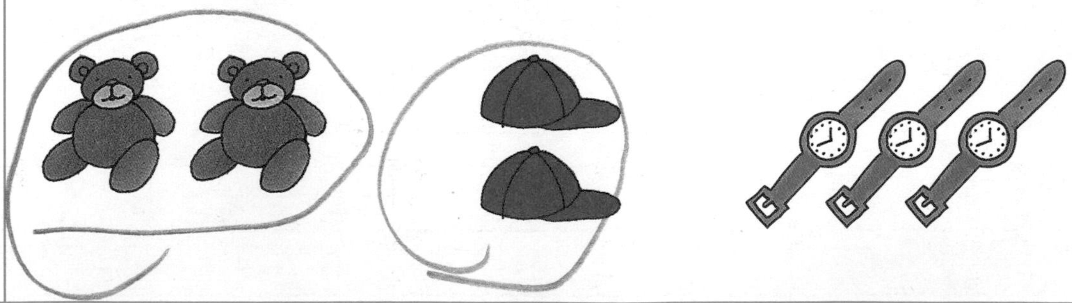

5.

5
five

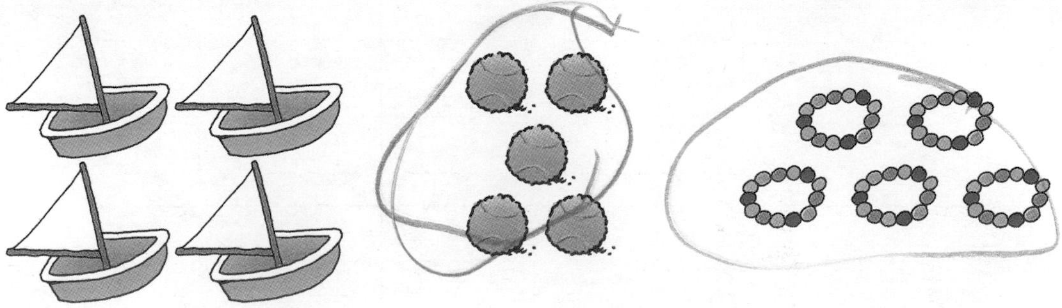

Count. Write the numbers.

1.

one

2.

two

3.

three

4.

four

5.

five

 Home Connection Children need many opportunities to show numbers. Place some rice on a cookie sheet. Give your child a number between 1 and 5 and have him or her write that number in the rice.

five   5

Count. Write how many.
Look for a pattern.

1.

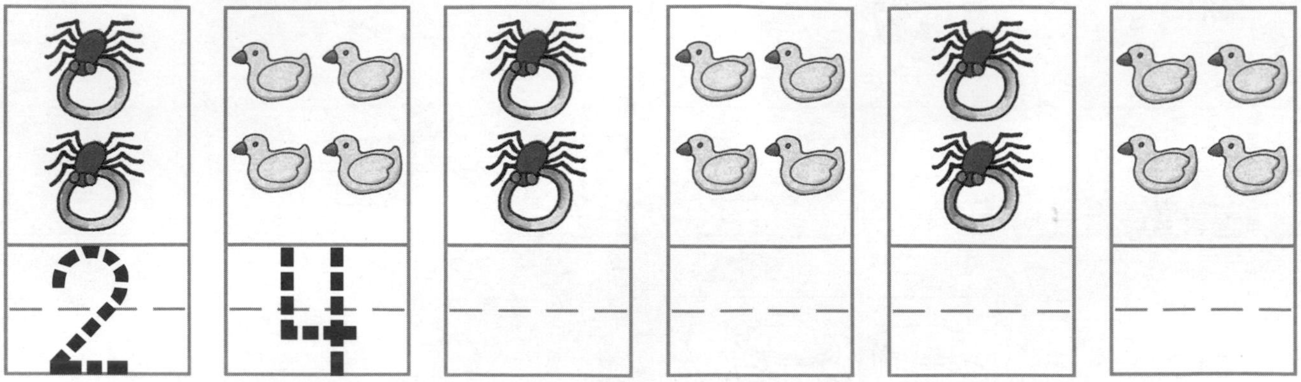

2	4				

2.

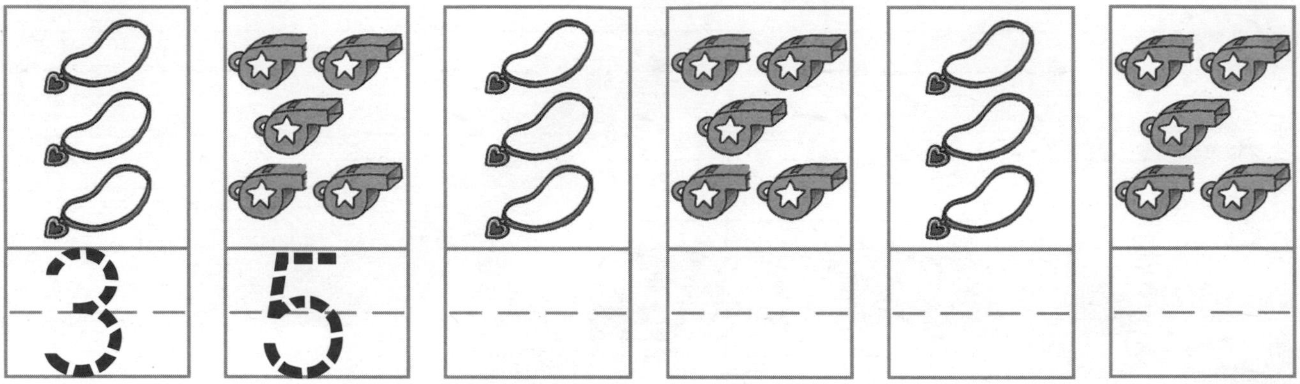

3	5				

3.

1	2				

4.

Make
Your
Own

© Silver Burdett Ginn Inc. All rights reserved.

There are zero children.

1. Write the number.

zero

2. Write how many children.

Home Connection Have your child show you which teacups show zero children. Then have your child think of items of which there are zero in your home: for example, live elephants.

seven   **7**

Write how many.

1.

   4

2.

3.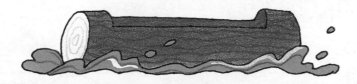

4.

 Problem Solving

Journal Idea

 Sam has 0 ride tickets.
Can he go on any rides?
Tell why or why not.

© Silver Burdett Ginn Inc. All rights

Name_____

Problem Solving
Make a Graph

STRATEGY
Understand
Plan
Solve
Look Back

How many balloons are in each color?

 Understand

You need to find how many , , and .

 Plan

You can make a graph.

Word Bank

graph

 Solve

Look at the picture.
Color the balloons in the graph.

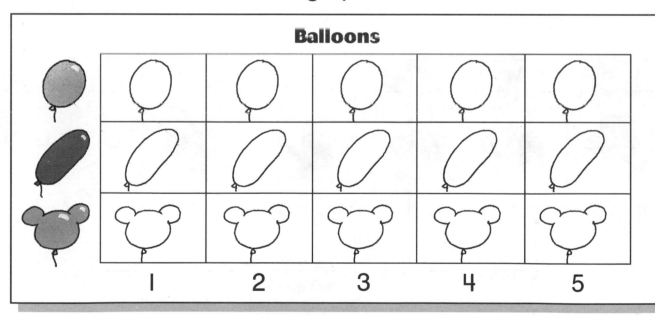

Balloons

| | 1 | 2 | 3 | 4 | 5 |

How many of each are there?

 _ _ _ _ _ _ _ _   _ _ _ _ _ _ _ _   _ _ _ _ _ _ _ _

 Look Back

Do your answers make sense?

 Home Connection Pictographs can help children count objects. Pick some simple objects in your house and help your child make a pictograph to show how many.

1. Use the picture to make a graph.
   Color to show how many of each.

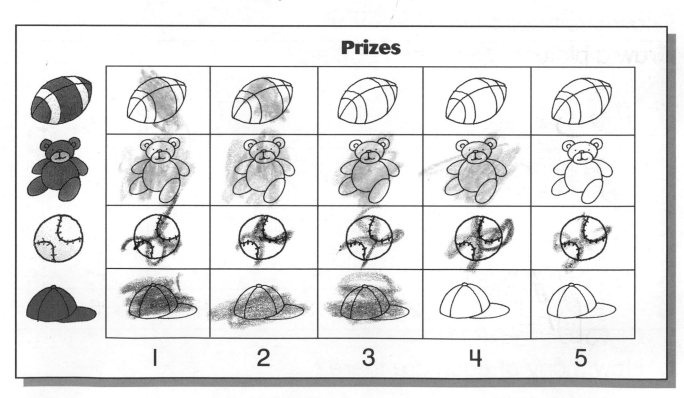

Prizes

2. How many of each are there?

 _____

 _____

 _____

Name_____ **Ways to Show Numbers**

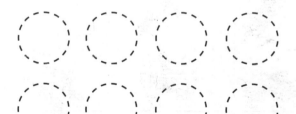

Show each number with ● .
Draw a picture. Write the number.

1.

eight

○ ○ ○ ○
○ ○ ○ ○

8

2.

five

3.

three

 Home Connection Encourage your child to talk about the different ways to show numbers. Have your child show numbers 1 to 12 in different ways.

nineteen   **19**

Draw and write.

	Word	Picture	Number
1.	ten	○ ○ ○ ○ ○ ○ ○ ○ ○ ○	10
2.	four		
3.	six		
4.	eleven		
5.			

Make Your Own

© Silver Burdett Ginn Inc. All rights reserved.

5

7 is greater than 5.
5 is less than 7.

7

Write how many.
Circle the greater number.

Word Bank

greater
less

1.

3   5

2.

⑫   8

3.

5   ⑨

4.

4   ⑥

Home Connection Give your child two groups of pennies with 12 or less in each group. Have him or her tell you how many in each group and which number is greater.

twenty-one   **21**

Write each number.
Circle the number that is less.

1.

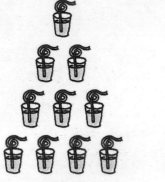

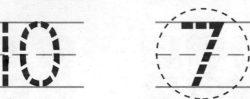

10   7

2.

_____
- - - - - - -
_____

3.

_____
- - - - - - -
_____

4.

_____
- - - - - - -
_____

© Silver Burdett Ginn Inc. All rights reserved.

What Do You Think?

Journal Idea

 8 is greater than 5. What is another number that is greater than 5?

0	1	2	3	4

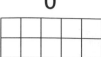 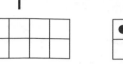 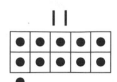 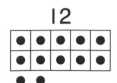 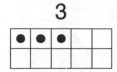

5	6	7	8	9

10	11	12

Word Bank

before
after
between

2 comes before 3.
3 comes after 2.
3 comes between 2 and 4.

Write each missing number.

1.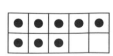

    5   _ _ _ _

2.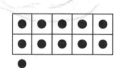

    _ _ _ _   12

3.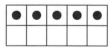

    _ _ _ _   9

4.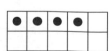

    _ _ _ _   3   _ _ _ _

🏠 **Home Connection** Play a guessing game with your child. For example,
"I am thinking of the number that comes before 6. What number is this?"

twenty-three   **23**

Write each missing number.

Before	After	Between
1. __2__ , 3	5, __6__	6, __7__ , 8
2. __7__ , 8	11, __12__	0, __1__ , 2
3. __0__ , 1	9, __10__	10, __11__ , 12
4. __5__ , 6	4, __5__	5, __6__ , 7
5. __3__ , 4, __5__ , 6, __7__ , __8__ , 9

© Silver Burdett Ginn Inc. All rights reserved.

Name_____

Think: Color to show the pattern.
What comes next?

Word Bank
pattern

1.

2.

3.

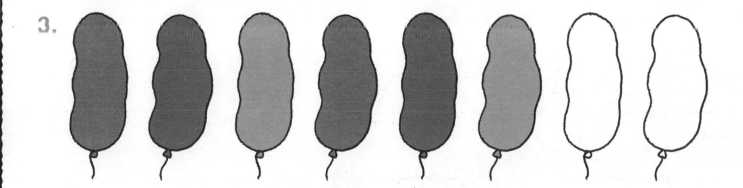

4.

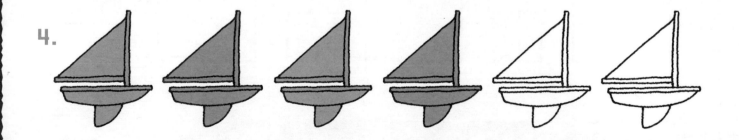

5.

 Home Connection Ask your child to tell you about each pattern. Then have your child make a pattern with household objects such as forks and spoons.

Draw and color to show a pattern.

1.

2.

3.

4.

5.

What Do You Think?

Journal Idea

What if you have only 1 crayon?
What pattern could you make?
Draw and color a pattern.

© Silver Burdett Ginn Inc. All rights reserved

first second third fourth fifth sixth seventh eighth ninth tenth

Circle the correct place.

1.

second

(third)

fourth

2.

third

fourth

(fifth)

3.

(first)

fifth

seventh

4.

ninth

(seventh)

sixth

5.

tenth

first

(fourth)

6.

(eighth)

sixth

fourth

7.

(sixth)

ninth

third

8.

second

tenth

(seventh)

9.

eighth

third

(second)

Home Connection Discuss with your child the order in which the
steps of a task are done. For example, when putting on socks and shoes,
"First, I put on my socks. Second, I put on my shoes. Third, I tie my laces."

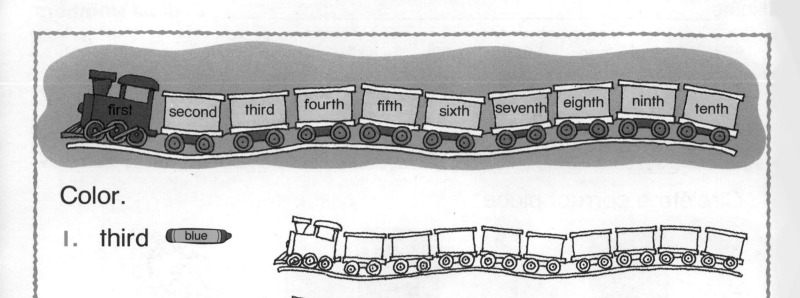

first second third fourth fifth sixth seventh eighth ninth tenth

Color.

1. third 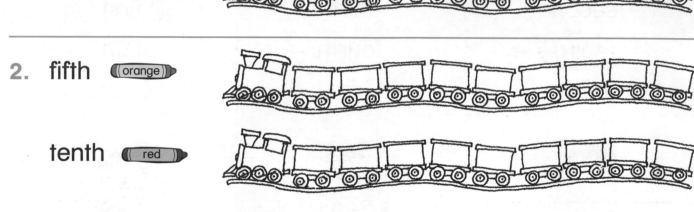 blue

   seventh green

2. fifth orange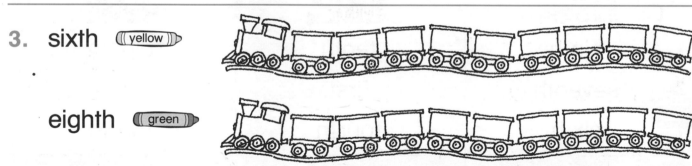

   tenth red

3. sixth yellow

   eighth green

PROBLEM SOLVING

Problem Solving

4. Bob is first in line.
   Tina is farthest from Bob.
   Brian is next to Tina.
   Jane is between Brian and Bob.
   Name the children in order.

© Silver Burdett Ginn Inc. All rights reserved.

Name_____

1. Write the missing numbers.

   I, _____ , 3, _____ , 5, _____ , 7, _____

2. Write each number. Circle the greater number.

   _____      _____

3. Color to show the pattern.

4. Color to show each place.

   third ⬤ red   fifth ⬤ yellow   ninth ⬤ green

5. Use the graph. Write how many.

   Favorite Food

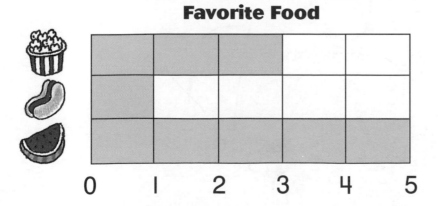

   0   I   2   3   4   5

   _____

Name_____ **Extra Practice**

1. Color each group.

   3  red

   6 blue

   2 green

2. Start at 0.
   Connect the dots in order.

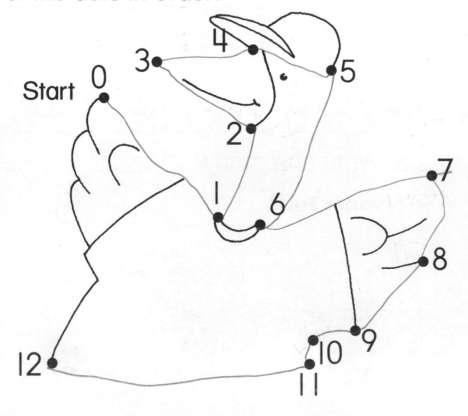

© Silver Burdett Ginn Inc. All rights reserved.

Name_____

1. Draw a group to show 1 fewer.
    Draw a group to show 1 more.

I fewer	I more

2. Circle the groups that show 9.

3. Color the third (yellow) and the eighth (orange).

4. Color to show the pattern.

What You Need

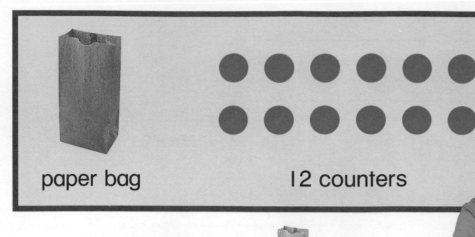

paper bag   12 counters

① Put all the ● in the 🛍.
② Take some out.
   Draw and write how many.
③ Draw and write to show 1 more.

How many	1 more
1.	
2.	
3.	

For Your Portfolio
You might put this page in your portfolio.

The Bug Book

written by Leslie Barna

illustrated by Liisa Guida

This Math Storybook

belongs to

A

One big ladybug
sits in a tree.

Two more join her.
Now there are three.

© Silver Burdett Ginn Inc. All rights reserved.

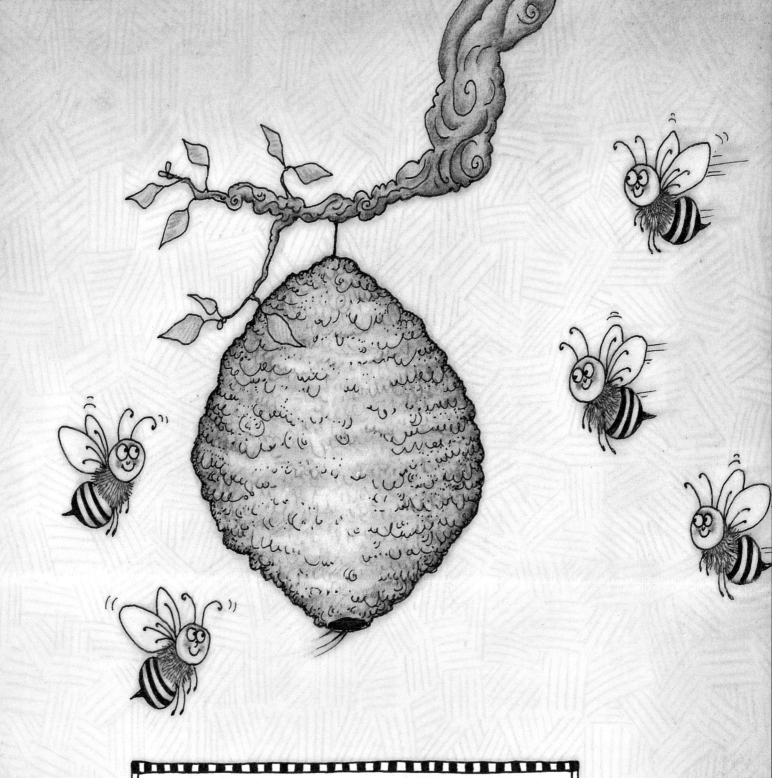

Two little bumblebees
fly near a hive.

Three more join them.
Now there are five. 5

One bug is all alone.
What will she do?

One more joins her.
Now there are two.

© Silver Burdett Ginn Inc. All rights reserved.

Three happy butterflies
smile as they wait.

Five more join them.
Now there are eight.

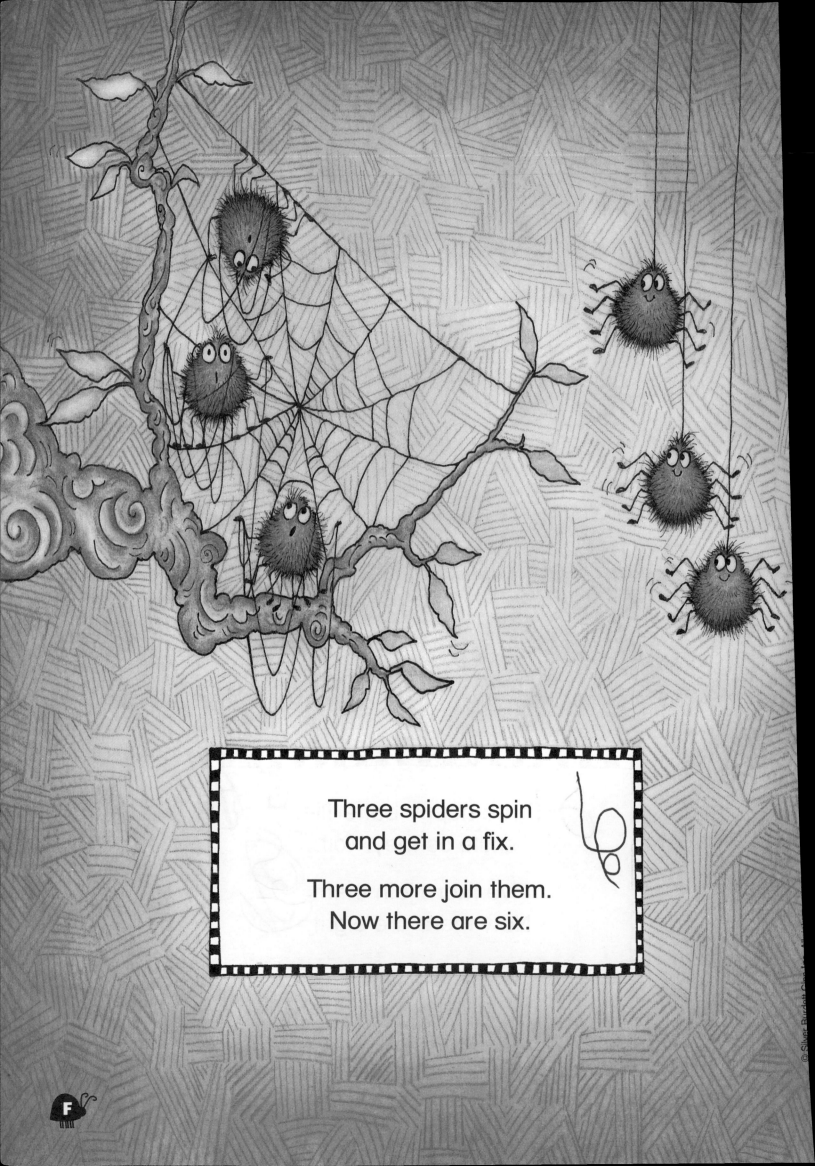

Three spiders spin
and get in a fix.

Three more join them.
Now there are six.

Draw some bugs
for all to see.

If two more join them,
how many will there be?

G

A Note to the Family

Here are some learning ideas you can share with your child.

 Enjoy The Bug Book Together

- Read each page with your child. Ask your child to count the number of bugs in each group on the page. Then talk about how to find how many there are in all. Show your child how to write an addition sentence.

  For example: 1 big ladybug and 2 little ladybugs are 3 in all
  $$1 + 2 = 3$$

- Encourage your child to show you what she or he drew on the last page of *The Bug Book*. Ask your child how many bugs there would be if three more flew into the picture.

 At-Home Activity

- Make "Edible Ants on a Log" to help your child practice addition. You will need pieces of celery filled with peanut butter for the logs and raisins for the ants. Say a number between 0 and 6 and tell your child to place that many "ants" on the log. Then name a second number of ants to put on the log. Ask "How many ants are there in all?" Make several logs so that the activity can be repeated. The logs make good treats for the entire family!

 Read More About It!

To read more stories about addition with your child, look for the following books in your local library.

- *Anno's Counting House* by Mitsumasa Anno (Putnam, 1982)
- *One Gorilla* by Atsuko Morozumi (Farrar, Straus & Giroux, 1990)
- *So Many Cats!* by Beatrice Schenk de Regniers (Clarion Books, 1985)

 Visit Our Web Site!

INTERNET ACTIVITY
www.sbgmath.com

H

Use counters to tell addition stories.
Then draw or write one story.

Home Connection Using counters to show number stories gives children a chance to show what they know about adding. Help your child make up addition stories and solve them together.

Solve.
Use counters if you like.

1. 3 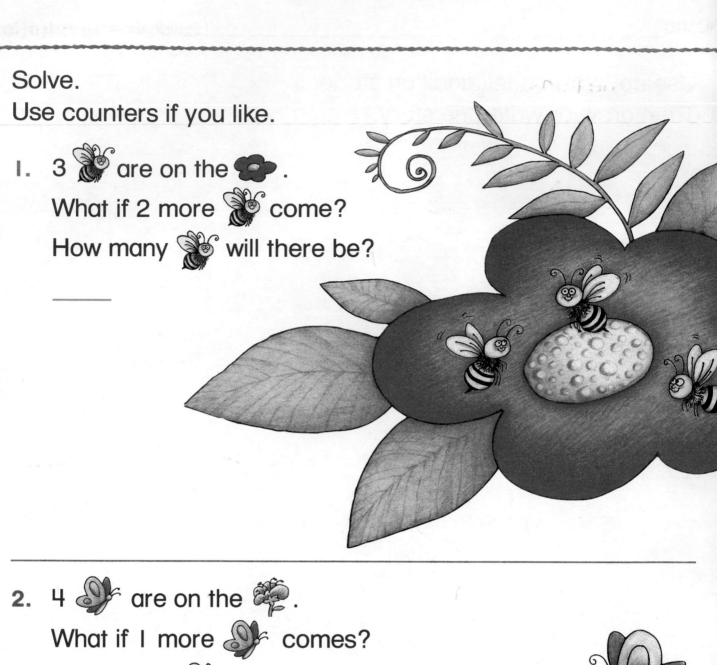 are on the ❀ .
   What if 2 more come?
   How many will there be?

   ____

2. 4 are on the .
   What if 1 more comes?
   How many will there be?

   ____

Name_____**Using Pictures to Add**

Write the numbers.

1. 　　　　

   2　and　**2**　are　**4** in all
   ___　　　　　　___　　　　___

2. 　　　　

   _____　and　_____　are　_____ in all

3.

   _____　and　_____　are　_____ in all

4.

   _____　and　_____　are　_____ in all

5.

   _____　and　_____　are　_____ in all

6.

   _____　and　_____　are　_____ in all

7. 　　　　

   _____　and　_____　are　_____ in all

Home Connection Pictures can help children add. Ask your child to draw simple pictures to make up addition stories.

forty-one　　**41**

Draw to show each number.
Write how many.

1.

2   and   3   are ____ in all

2.

4   and   1   are ____ altogether

3. Draw 2 groups. Write how many.

____ and ____ are ____ in all

Make Your Own

© Silver Burdett Ginn Inc. All rights reserved.

I can make sums for 3 in many ways.

● ● ●	$0 + 3 = 3$
● ● ●	$1 + 2 = 3$
● ● ●	$2 + 1 = 3$
● ● ●	$3 + 0 = 3$

How many ways can you make 5?
Use counters. Color.
Write each addition sentence.
Look for a pattern.

Word Bank
addition sentence

1. ○ ○ ○ ○ ○   ___ + ___ – ___

2. ○ ○ ○ ○ ○   ___ + ___ = ___

3. ○ ○ ○ ○ ○   ___ + ___ = ___

4. ○ ○ ○ ○ ○   ___ + ___ = ___

5. ○ ○ ○ ○ ○   ___ + ___ = ___

6. ○ ○ ○ ○ ○   ___ + ___ = ___

Home Connection Review the different ways to show sums for 5 and 6. Encourage your child to write sums for other numbers.

forty-five **45**

How many ways can you make 6?
Use counters. Color.
Write each addition sentence.

1. ○○○○○○   ____ + ____ = ____

2. ○○○○○○   ____ + ____ = ____

3. ○○○○○○   ____ + ____ = ____

4. ○○○○○○   ____ + ____ = ____

5. ○○○○○○   ____ + ____ = ____

6. ○○○○○○   ____ + ____ = ____

7. ○○○○○○   ____ + ____ = ____

 Critical Thinking Corner

Number Sense **Journal Idea**

 Are there more ways to
make 4 or to make 6?
Tell why. Then try it.

Use counters to show ways to make 7.
Color. Write the addition sentence.

1.

___ + ___ = ___

2.

___ + ___ = ___

3. ◯ ◯ ◯ ◯ ◯ ◯ ◯

___ + ___ = ___

4. ◯ ◯ ◯ ◯ ◯ ◯ ◯

___ + ___ = ___

5. ◯ ◯ ◯ ◯ ◯ ◯ ◯

___ + ___ = ___

6. ◯ ◯ ◯ ◯ ◯ ◯ ◯

___ + ___ = ___

Home Connection Review the different ways to show sums
for 7 and 8. Encourage your child to write sums for other numbers.

Use counters to show ways to make 8.
Color. Write the addition sentence.

1.

___ + ___ = ___

2.

___ + ___ = ___

3.

___ + ___ = ___

 Checkpoint

1. Use counters. Add.

3 ⬤   and   1 ⬤   ___ altogether

Write the numbers.

2.

___ and   ___ are   ___ in all

3.

___ + ___ = ___

You can add across. You can add down.

$$3 + 2 = 5$$

$$\begin{array}{r} 3 \\ + \ 2 \\ \hline 5 \end{array}$$

Write the numbers. Add.

1.

$$\begin{array}{r} \\ + \\ \hline \end{array}$$

_____ + _____ = _____

2.

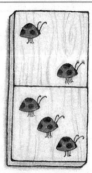

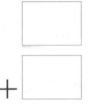

_____ + _____ = _____

3.

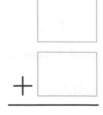

_____ + _____ = _____

4.

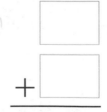

_____ + _____ = _____

Home Connection Show two groups of objects such as beans or pasta. Ask your child to add by writing the problem horizontally and vertically. Discuss the similarities and differences.

Follow the path to the 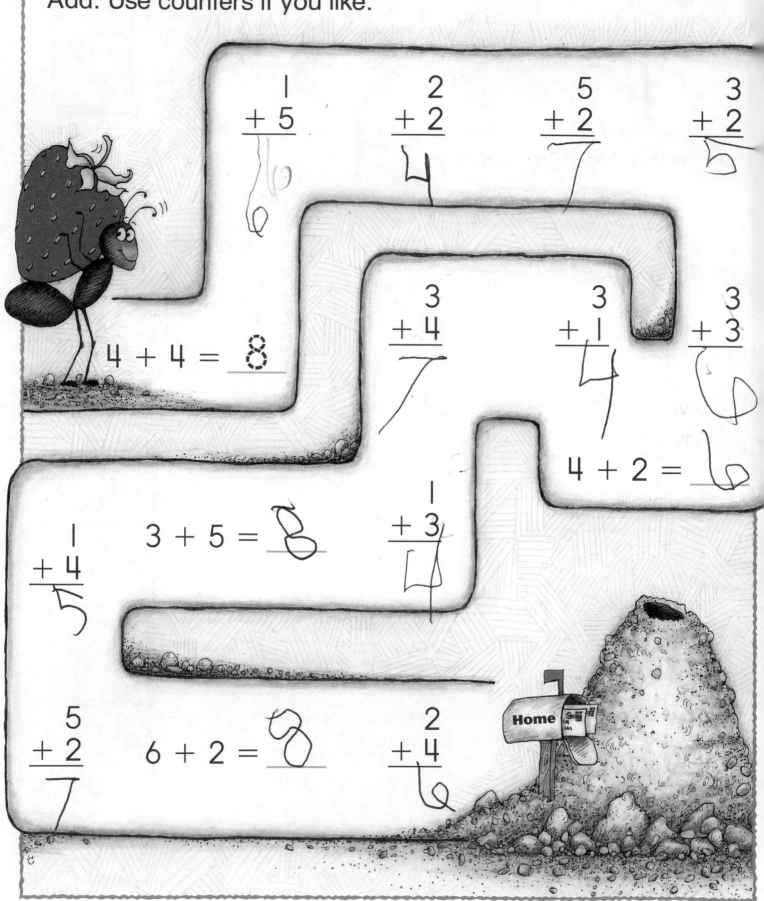 home.
Add. Use counters if you like.

$\begin{array}{r} 1 \\ + 5 \\ \hline 6 \end{array}$

$\begin{array}{r} 2 \\ + 2 \\ \hline 4 \end{array}$

$\begin{array}{r} 5 \\ + 2 \\ \hline 7 \end{array}$

$\begin{array}{r} 3 \\ + 2 \\ \hline 5 \end{array}$

$4 + 4 = 8$

$\begin{array}{r} 3 \\ + 4 \\ \hline 7 \end{array}$

$\begin{array}{r} 3 \\ + 1 \\ \hline 4 \end{array}$

$\begin{array}{r} 3 \\ + 3 \\ \hline 6 \end{array}$

$4 + 2 = 6$

$\begin{array}{r} 1 \\ + 4 \\ \hline 5 \end{array}$

$3 + 5 = 8$

$\begin{array}{r} 1 \\ + 3 \\ \hline 4 \end{array}$

$\begin{array}{r} 5 \\ + 2 \\ \hline 7 \end{array}$

$6 + 2 = 8$

$\begin{array}{r} 2 \\ + 4 \\ \hline 6 \end{array}$

Home

Solve.
Draw a picture or write an addition sentence.

1. 2 crawl.

    3 more come.

    How many are there in all? _____

2. 3 fly.

    4 more join them.

    How many are there altogether? _____

3. 2 buzz.

    2 more join them.

    How many are there in all? _____

Home Connection Encourage your child to talk about the different ways to solve addition problems. Make up some problems for your child to solve.

fifty-one   51

1. Ask 5 friends how they like to add.
   Color a box to show each friend's way.

How We Like to Add

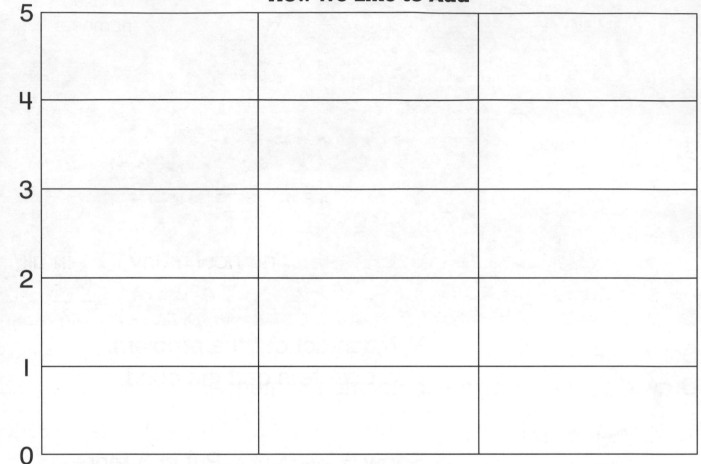

5			
4			
3			
2			
1			
0	Use counters	Use pictures	Use numbers

$2 + 5 = 7$

 Critical Thinking Corner

Number Sense

2. Share your graph with a friend.
   Tell how your graphs are the same.
   Tell how they are different.

© Silver Burdett Ginn Inc. All rights

Problem Solving
Act It Out
STRATEGY
Understand
Plan
Look Back
Solve

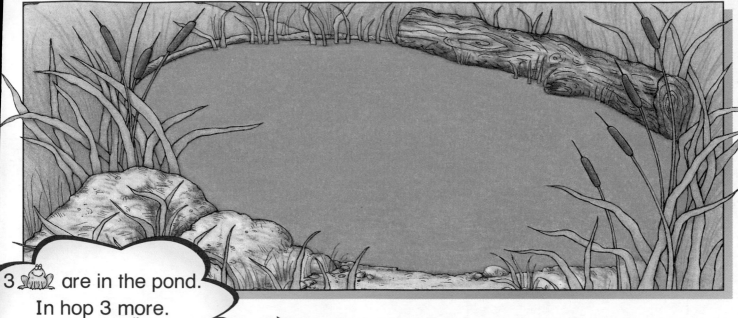

3 are in the pond.
In hop 3 more.
How many are
there in all?

Understand

You need to find how many in all.

Plan

You can act out the problem.
Use counters and the pond.

Solve

Show 3 counters. Put in 3 more.

There are 6 in all.

Look Back

Did you answer the question?

Use counters to solve.

1. On the log are 2 🦋.

   2 more are on the rock.

   How many 🦋 are there

   altogether? __4__

2. 2 🦆 are in the pond.

   3 more join them.

   How many 🦆 are there

   now? _____

 Home Connection Children can use counters or common household objects to act out a problem. Make up some problems for your child to act out.

Use counters to act out the number story.
Write the numbers.

The Bug Picnic

I 🐜 crawls onto the ▨.

I 🐝 flies in to join it.

Now, how many bugs are there? _____

Next, 2 🐞 come to the picnic.

Now, how many bugs are there? _____

I 🦗 hops over.

Now, how many bugs are there? _____

3 🐛 crawl over.

How many bugs are there in all? _____

© Silver Burdett Ginn Inc. All rights reserved.

What happens when you add zero?

Use counters and the ⬚.
Solve.

1. Put in 2 ⬤.
   Put in 0.
   How many are there
   altogether? __2__

2. Put in 8 ⬤.
   Put in 0.
   How many are there
   altogether? __8__

3. Put in 7 ⬤.
   Put in 0.
   How many are there
   in all? __7__

4. Put in 5 ⬤.
   Put in 0.
   How many are there
   now? __5__

5. Put in 1 ⬤.
   Put in 0.
   How many are there
   now? __1__

6. Put in 6 ⬤.
   Put in 0.
   How many are there
   in all? __6__

Home Connection When 0 is added to any number, the sum is the same as that number. Ask your child, "How much is one million and one plus zero?" and similar questions with very large numbers.

Add. Use counters if you like.
Look for facts with zero.

1.
$$\begin{array}{r} 0 \\ +\ 2 \\ \hline \end{array}$$ 2
$$\begin{array}{r} 1 \\ +\ 3 \\ \hline \end{array}$$ 4
$$\begin{array}{r} 5 \\ +\ 2 \\ \hline \end{array}$$ 7
$$\begin{array}{r} 3 \\ +\ 0 \\ \hline \end{array}$$ 3
$$\begin{array}{r} 0 \\ +\ 4 \\ \hline \end{array}$$ 4
$$\begin{array}{r} 3 \\ +\ 3 \\ \hline \end{array}$$ 6

2.
$$\begin{array}{r} 2 \\ +\ 2 \\ \hline \end{array}$$ 4
$$\begin{array}{r} 0 \\ +\ 0 \\ \hline \end{array}$$ 0
$$\begin{array}{r} 1 \\ +\ 4 \\ \hline \end{array}$$ 5
$$\begin{array}{r} 4 \\ +\ 0 \\ \hline \end{array}$$ 4
$$\begin{array}{r} 0 \\ +\ 1 \\ \hline \end{array}$$ 1
$$\begin{array}{r} 0 \\ +\ 7 \\ \hline \end{array}$$ 7

3.
$$\begin{array}{r} 0 \\ +\ 4 \\ \hline \end{array}$$ 4
$$\begin{array}{r} 4 \\ +\ 2 \\ \hline \end{array}$$ 6
$$\begin{array}{r} 7 \\ +\ 0 \\ \hline \end{array}$$ 7
$$\begin{array}{r} 3 \\ +\ 2 \\ \hline \end{array}$$ 5
$$\begin{array}{r} 6 \\ +\ 0 \\ \hline \end{array}$$ 6
$$\begin{array}{r} 0 \\ +\ 3 \\ \hline \end{array}$$ 3

4. $0 + 6 = $ 6 $7 + 1 = $ 8 $0 + 7 = $ 7

5. $4 + 3 = $ 7 $0 + 5 = $ 5 $8 + 0 = $ 8

What Do You Think?

Journal Idea

I think that 0 is the easiest number in the
world to add. Do you? Why or why not?

© Silver Burdett Ginn Inc. All rights

Name_____

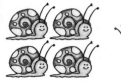

$4 + 1 = \underline{5}$ $1 + 4 = \underline{5}$

Use counters.
Write each sum.

1. $4 + 3 = \underline{7}$

   $3 + 4 = \underline{7}$

2. $5 + 1 = \underline{6}$

   $1 + 5 = \underline{6}$

3. $1 + 3 = \underline{4}$

   $3 + 1 = \underline{4}$

4. $6 + 1 = \underline{7}$

   $1 + 6 = \underline{7}$

5. $5 + 2 = \underline{7}$

   $2 + 5 = \underline{7}$

6. $3 + 2 = \underline{5}$

   $2 + 3 = \underline{5}$

7. $5 + 3 = \underline{8}$

   $3 + 5 = \underline{8}$

8. $7 + 1 = \underline{8}$

   $1 + 7 = \underline{8}$

Home Connection The order in which two numbers are added
does not change the sum. Give your child some addition examples. Have
him or her change the order of the numbers and find each answer.

Add. Then change the order.
Use counters if you like.

1.
$$\begin{array}{r} 1 \\ + 2 \\ \hline 3 \end{array}$$
$$\begin{array}{r} \boxed{2} \\ + \boxed{1} \\ \hline 3 \end{array}$$

2.
$$\begin{array}{r} 3 \\ + 2 \\ \hline 5 \end{array}$$
$$\begin{array}{r} \boxed{5} \\ + \boxed{2} \\ \hline 7 \end{array}$$

3.
$$\begin{array}{r} 0 \\ + 4 \\ \hline 4 \end{array}$$
$$\begin{array}{r} \boxed{4} \\ + \boxed{0} \\ \hline 4 \end{array}$$

4.
$$\begin{array}{r} 6 \\ + 2 \\ \hline 8 \end{array}$$
$$\begin{array}{r} \boxed{8} \\ + \boxed{2} \\ \hline 10 \end{array}$$

5.
$$\begin{array}{r} 2 \\ + 4 \\ \hline 6 \end{array}$$
$$\begin{array}{r} \boxed{4} \\ + \boxed{2} \\ \hline 6 \end{array}$$

6.
$$\begin{array}{r} 1 \\ + 6 \\ \hline 7 \end{array}$$
$$\begin{array}{r} \boxed{7} \\ + \boxed{1} \\ \hline 8 \end{array}$$

Problem Solving

7. Look at the picture.
    How many are there in all?
    Write two addition sentences.

_____ + _____ = _____

_____ + _____ = _____

© Silver Burdett Ginn

Problem Solving
Use Data From a Picture

APPLICATION
Understand
Plan
Look Back
Solve

Use the picture to solve each problem.
Think: What do you need to find out?

1. There are 2 🐝.
   There are 4 🦋.
   How many are there
   in all? 6

2. There are 4 🐞.
   There is 1 🐜.
   How many are there
   altogether? 5

3. There are 3 🐢.
   There are 3 🐰.
   How many are there
   in all? 6

4. There are 2 🐦.
   There are 3 🐢.
   How many are there
   in all? 5

5. There are 4 🦋.
   There are 4 🐞.
   How many are there
   in all? 8

6. There is 1 🐜.
   There are 2 🐝.
   How many are there
   altogether? 3

Home Connection Show your child a magazine picture. Help
her or him make up and solve addition problems about the scene.

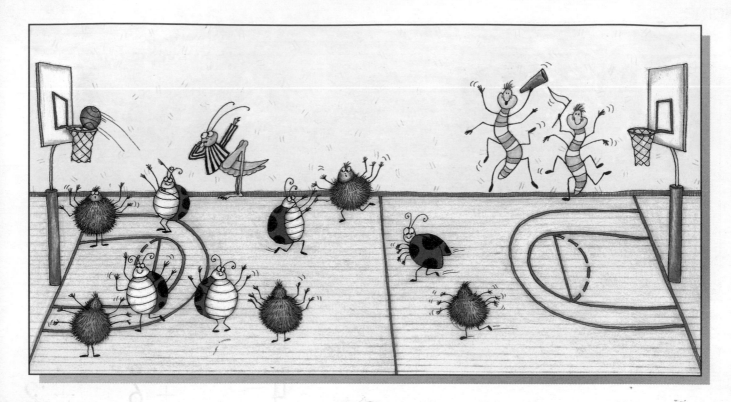

Make Your Own

Look at the picture.
What number stories can you tell?
Draw or write two stories below.

1. 5 0 red bugs and 5 brown bugs.

2.

Name_____

Write each addition sentence.

1.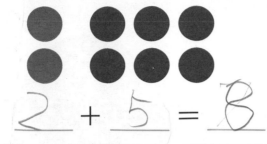

$\underline{2} + \underline{5} = \underline{8}$

2.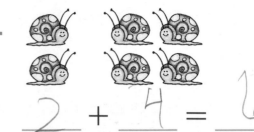

$\underline{2} + \underline{4} = \underline{6}$

3. Use and 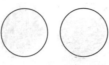. Color to make 6.
   Write the addition sentence.

 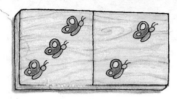 $\underline{3} + \underline{3} = \underline{6}$

4. Write the numbers. Add.

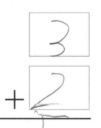

$\underline{3} + \underline{2} = \underline{5}$

$\begin{array}{r} 3 \\ + 2 \\ \hline 5 \end{array}$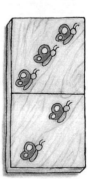

5. Add.

$\begin{array}{r} 5 \\ + 2 \\ \hline 7 \end{array}$
$\begin{array}{r} 2 \\ + 5 \\ \hline 7 \end{array}$
$\begin{array}{r} 3 \\ + 0 \\ \hline 3 \end{array}$
$\begin{array}{r} 0 \\ + 3 \\ \hline 3 \end{array}$
$\begin{array}{r} 2 \\ + 4 \\ \hline 6 \end{array}$
$\begin{array}{r} 4 \\ + 2 \\ \hline 6 \end{array}$

6. Use the picture to solve.

There are $\underline{4}$ .
There are $\underline{2}$ .
How many are there in all?

$\underline{6}$

Name_____ **Performance Assessment**

What You Need

| paper bag | red and yellow counters | Workmat 4 |

① Put the counters in the . Shake.

② Take some counters out.

③ Sort the counters on .

④ Write an addition sentence below.

⑤ Repeat steps 1 – 4.

1.

___ + ___ = ___

2.

___ + ___ = ___

3.

___ + ___ = ___

4.

___ + ___ = ___

5.

___ + ___ = ___

6.

___ + ___ = ___

 For Your Portfolio

You might put this page in your portfolio.

© Silver Burdett Ginn Inc. All rights reserved

Use counters to tell subtraction stories
about children in the park.
Draw or write one story.

**...me Connection** Give yo................... buttons, pennies, or socks. Ask your child to ....ories.

Solve. Use counters if you like.

1. 2 children are on the  .

   What if one goes away?

   How many will there be? __1__

2. 4 children are on the .

   What if 2 go away?

   How many will there be? __2__

Name_____

Look at the cube train.
Write how many of each color.
Complete each subtraction sentence.

Word Bank

subtraction sentence

1.

_2_ and _3_

$5 - 3 = $ _2_

$5 - 2 = $ _3_

2.

_1_ and _4_

$5 - 4 = $ _1_

$5 - 1 = $ _4_

3.

_5_ and _0_

$5 - 0 = $ _5_

$5 - 5 = $ _0_

Home Connection To help your child practice subtracting, put
5 or 6 pennies or other household items in your hand. Take some out.
Ask your child how many are still in your hand. Then count them together.

seventy-five   **75**

Look at the cube train.
Write how many of each color.
Complete each subtraction sentence.

1.

__4__ and __2__

$6 - \underline{2} = \underline{4}$

$6 - \underline{4} = \underline{2}$

2.

____ and ____

$6 - \underline{} = \underline{}$

$6 - \underline{} = \underline{}$

3.

____ and ____

$6 - \underline{} = \underline{}$

4.

____ and ____

$6 - \underline{} = \underline{}$

$6 - \underline{} = \underline{}$

© Silver Burdett Ginn Inc. All rights reserved

Name_____

Use two colors of 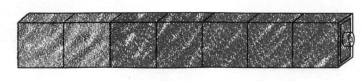 to show ways
to make 7. Color.
Write the subtraction sentences.

1.

_2_ and _5_

$7 - 5 = 2$

$7 - 2 = 5$

2.

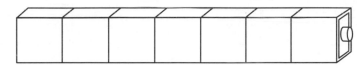

____ and ____

___ – ___ = ___

___ – ___ = ___

3.

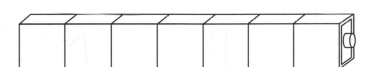

____ and ____

___ – ___ = ___

___ – ___ = ___

4.

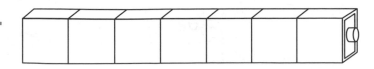

____ and ____

___ – ___ = ___

___ – ___ = ___

Use two colors of  to show ways
to make 8. Color.
Write the subtraction sentences.

1.

_____ — _____ = _____

_____ and _____   _____ — _____ = _____

2.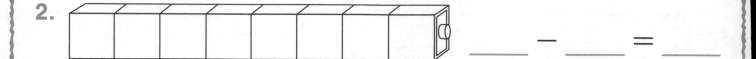

_____ — _____ = _____

_____ and _____   _____ — _____ = _____

3.

_____ — _____ = _____

_____ and _____   _____ — _____ = _____

4.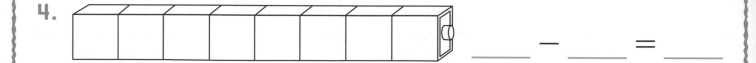

_____ — _____ = _____

_____ and _____   _____ — _____ = _____

5.

_____ — _____ = _____

_____ and _____   _____ — _____ = _____

© Silver Burdett Ginn Inc. All rights

Name_____

There are 4 children.
Then 1 goes home.
How many children
are left?

Understand

You need to find how
many children are left.

Plan

You can write a number sentence.

Solve

$$ \underline{4} - \underline{1} = \underline{3} \text{ children} $$

Look Back

Did you answer the question?

Write each number sentence.

1.

___ − ___ = ___

2.

___ − ___ = ___

Home Connection Act out simple math stories using common household items. Ask your child to write number sentences to go with each story.

seventy-nine   **79**

Write each number sentence.

1.

$$3 - 1 = 2$$

2.

$$5 - 1 = 4$$

3.

$$4 - 1 = 3$$

4.

$$2 - 2 = 0$$

5.

$$6 - 1 = 5$$

6.

$$\underline{} - \underline{} = \underline{}$$

7.   Draw a picture with some
going away.

Make
Your
Own

Write the subtraction sentence.

$$2 - 1 = 1$$

jumprpe

No dumprope

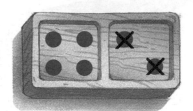 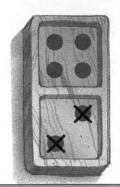 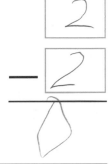

6 − 2 = 4

Write the numbers. Subtract.

1.

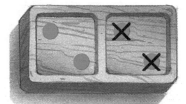 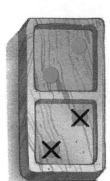 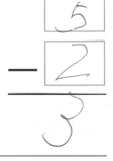

2 − 2 = 0

2.

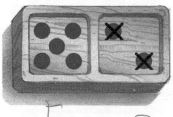  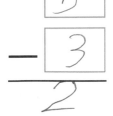

5 − 2 = 3

3.

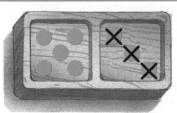 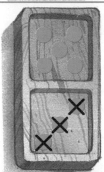 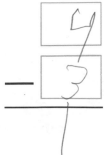

5 − 3 = 2

4.

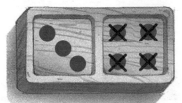 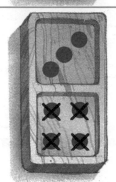

4 − 3 = 1

Connection Ask your child to place some small items such as beans or pennies across or down, make up a subtraction problem, and write it horizontally and vertically.

Find each difference.
Write the matching subtraction sentence.

1.
$$\begin{array}{r} 6 \\ -2 \\ \hline 4 \end{array}$$
6 – 2 = 4

2.
$$\begin{array}{r} 5 \\ -2 \\ \hline \end{array}$$
___ – ___ = ___

3.
$$\begin{array}{r} 4 \\ -2 \\ \hline \end{array}$$
___ – ___ = ___

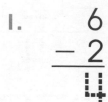

Checkpoint

Subtract.

1. 5 take away 3 ____ left

Cross out to subtract.

2.
4 – 2 = ____

3.
6 – 3 = ____

Write each number sentence.

4.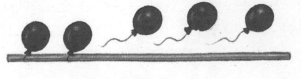
____ – ____ = ____

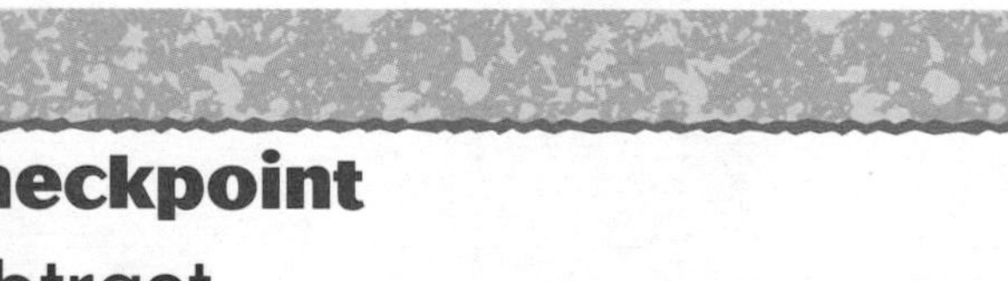

5.
____ – ____ = ____

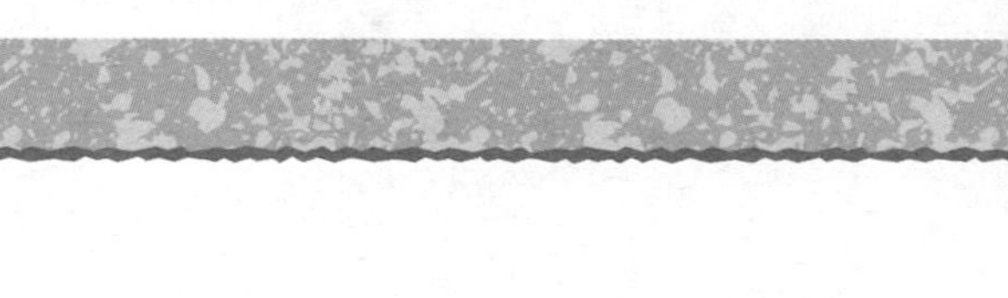

There are 6 🪁. 2 blow away.
How many 🪁 are left?
How can you solve this?

I used pictures.

I used counters.

I used numbers.

6-2=4

Solve. Draw or write to show how.

1. There are 5 .

   2 roll away.

   How many 🟤 are left? _____

2. There are 8 🚚 .

   Leon takes 4.

   How many 🚚 are left? _____

3. There are 6 🎈 .

   There a .

   How ma___re 🎈 are there? _____

🍎 **Home Connection** Make up a subtraction problem.
Encourage your child to show you different ways to solve it.

eighty-three 83

Solve.
Draw or write to show how.

1. 7   are sailing.

   2 sail away.

   How many are left?

   _____

2. There are 4 .

   3 roll away.

   How many are left?

   _____

3. There are 6  .

   4 blow away.

   How many are left?

   _____

4. 8  are flying.

   Some fly away.

   2 are left.

   How many  fly away? _____

Name_____ **Zero in Subtraction**

Use counters and the . Solve.

1. Show 3.
   Take away 3 to subtract.
   How many are left?

   _____

2. Show 5.
   Take away 5 to subtract.
   How many are
   there now?

   _____

3. Show 6.
   Take away 0 to subtract.
   How many are left?

   _____

4. Show 4.
   Take away 0 to subtract.
   How many are
   there now?

   _____

5. Show 8.
   Take away 8 to subtract.
   How many are
   there now?

   _____

6. Show 7.
   Take away 0 to subtract.
   How many are left?

   _____

 Home Connection Give your child buttons or other household items
to practice subtraction. Have him or her solve problems involving taking
away zero or taking away all to subtract; for example, 5 − 5 and 5 − 0.

eighty-five   **85**

Subtract.
Use counters if you like.

1.
5	2	7	4	5	6
− 0	− 2	− 2	− 0	− 4	− 6

5

2.
8	6	4	2	7	1
− 8	− 0	− 4	− 0	− 3	− 1

3.
7	8	5	7	3	7
− 0	− 3	− 5	− 4	− 0	− 7

4.
3	8	6	1	0	8
− 3	− 0	− 5	− 0	− 0	− 7

 Critical Thinking Corner

Number Sense   Journal Idea

 How is subtracting 0 like adding 0?

Write the numbers.
Then subtract.

I.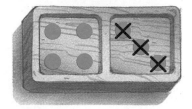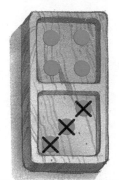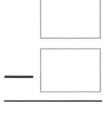

_____ − _____ = _____

2.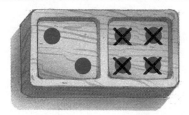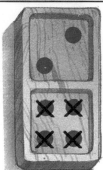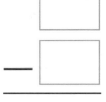

_____ − _____ = _____

3. Subtract.

$$\begin{array}{cccccc} 4 & 8 & 8 & 7 & 7 & 6 \\ -1 & -0 & -6 & -7 & -6 & -3 \end{array}$$

Add or subtract.
Write the number sentence.

4. 5 toys walk away.

add   subtract

_____ ◯ _____ = _____

5. 2 trucks come back.

add   subtract

_____ ◯ _____ = _____

Name_____ **Extra Practice**

Use counters. Play with a friend.

Roll the .

Write the subtraction sentence.

Move 1 space for each correct answer.

Start

1. _____ — _____ = _____

2. _____ — _____ = _____

3. _____ — _____ = _____

4. _____ — _____ = _____

5. _____ — _____ = _____

6. _____ — _____ = _____

7. _____ — _____ = _____

8. _____ — _____ = _____

9. _____ — _____ = _____

10. _____ — _____ = _____

End

© Silver Burdett Ginn Inc. All rights reserved.

Name_____

Write how many are left.

1. 5 minus 3 ____ left

2. 4 minus 3 ____ left

Cross out to subtract.

3.

8 − 5 = ____

4.

4 − 4 = ____

Subtract.

5. 5 − 3 = ____   7 − 6 = ____   3 − 0 = ____

6.
$$\begin{array}{r} 5 \\ -\ 0 \\ \hline \end{array} \qquad \begin{array}{r} 6 \\ -\ 6 \\ \hline \end{array} \qquad \begin{array}{r} 8 \\ -\ 4 \\ \hline \end{array} \qquad \begin{array}{r} 7 \\ -\ 3 \\ \hline \end{array} \qquad \begin{array}{r} 5 \\ -\ 4 \\ \hline \end{array} \qquad \begin{array}{r} 4 \\ -\ 2 \\ \hline \end{array}$$

Add or subtract.
Write the number sentence.

7. 4 fish join the others.

add   subtract

____ ◯ ____ = ____

8. I car leaves.

add   subtract

____ ◯ ____ = ____

Name_____ **Performance Assessment**

What You Need

Workmat 1

8 counters

1. Put some counters on the workmat.

2. Then take some away to subtract.

3. Write the number sentence below.

1.	2.
_____ − _____ = _____	_____ − _____ = _____
3.	4.
_____ − _____ = _____	_____ − _____ = _____

Do you have more or less after you subtract? Explain.

For Your Portfolio

You might put this page in your portfolio.

Name_____

How many toys are in the ?
Use counters.

1.   7 toys in all

_____ toys in the box

2.   3 toys in all

_____ toys in the box

3.   5 toys in all

_____ toys in the box

4.   6 toys in all

_____ toy in the box

5.   5 toys in all

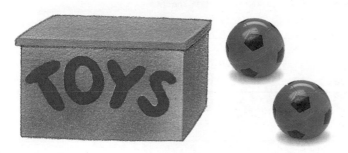

_____ toys in the box

6.   8 toys in all

_____ toys in the box

Use a . Press the keys.

Write the number you see.

1. Press ON/C   5   −   3   =   2

2. Press ON/C   7   −   2   =   5

3. Press ON/C   4   −   2   =   2

4. Press ON/C   3   −   3   =   0

5. Press ON/C   8   −   4   =   4

6. Press ON/C   6   −   0   =   6

© Silver Burdett Ginn Inc. All rights

Introducing Basic-Fact Strategies

Let's Go!

written by Shereen Gertel Rutman

illustrated by R.W. Alley

This Math Storybook
belongs to

Ashley

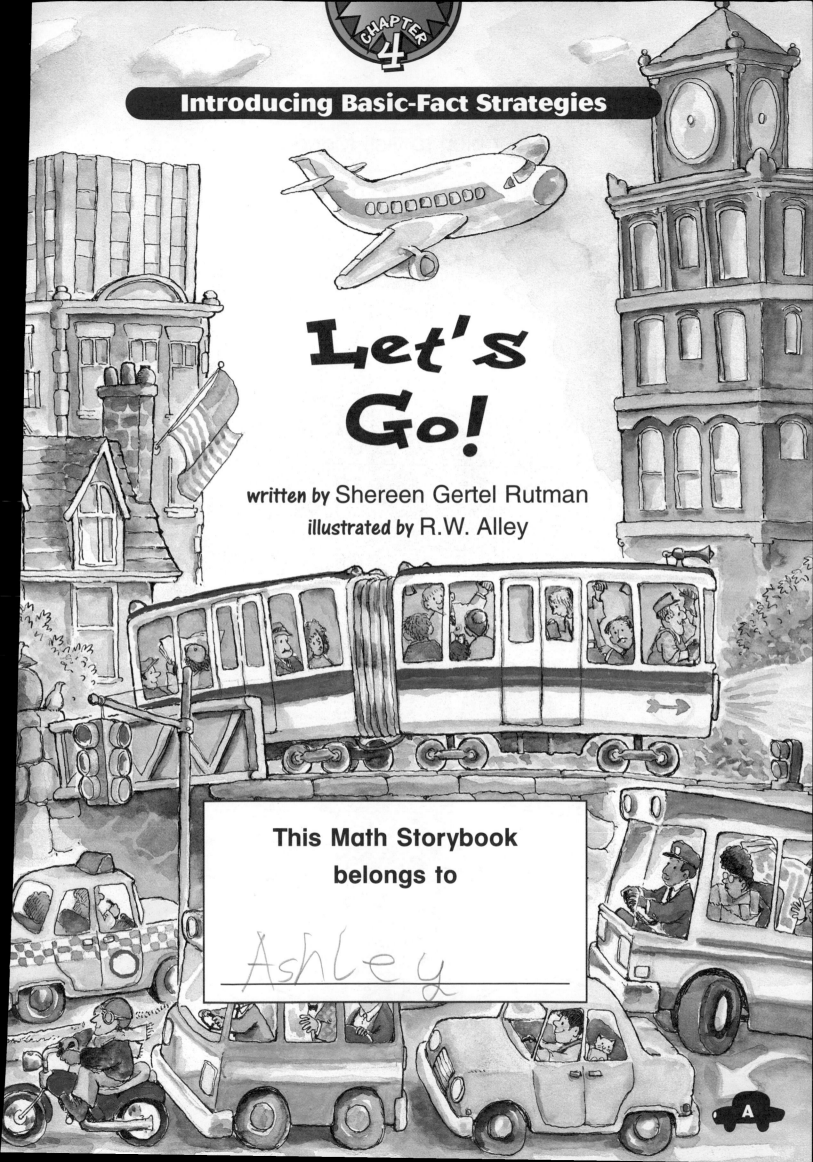

The Travel Club is on the way.
They plan to visit Mandalay.

We have 3 who are inside.
We have 2 who cannot ride.

Oh, no! Oh, no!

Maybe 5 can fit in a van!

© Silver Burdett Ginn Inc. All rights reserved.

B

Here come 4 more who we know.
5 + 4 makes 9 to go.

How can 9 fit in the van?
8 will fit. That leaves 1 man.

Oh, no! Oh, no!

Everybody out!

Here come 3 more. They are late!
9 + 3 makes 12 who wait.

Oh, no! Oh, no!

© Silver Burdett Ginn Inc. All rights reserved.

The 12 of us wait for the bus.
We line up but start to fuss.

We see that 8 have room to sit.
We see that 4 may not fit.

Oh, no! Oh, no!

We find 4 seats in the back row.
That means all of us can go.
8 + 4 makes 12, you know!

Let's go! Let's go!

© Silver Burdett Ginn Inc. All rights reserved.

Draw some friends who sit inside.
Draw some friends who wait outside.
Count your friends who go today
on this trip to Mandalay.

INTERNET ACTIVITY
www.sbgmath.com

A Note to the Family

**Here are some learning ideas
you can share with your child.**

 Enjoy *Let's Go!* Together

- Read each page of *Let's Go!* with your child. Ask your child to count the number of people on each page. Have your child tell addition and subtraction stories for each picture.

 At-Home Activities

- Make cookies or sandwiches using boat and car cookie cutters. Encourage your child to make up math problems using the shapes.
- Cut out pictures of vehicles from magazines with your child. Then have your child glue different numbers of pictures on several sheets of paper. Work together to write addition and subtraction stories for each sheet of pictures.

 Read More About It!

To read more math or theme-related stories with your child, look for the following books in your local library.

- *Freight Train* by Donald Crews (Morrow, 1992)
- *Red Fox and His Canoe* by Nathaniel Benchley (Harper, 1985)
- *Trucks You Can Count On* by Doug Magee (Putnam, 1986)
- *One, Two, Three, and Four. No More?* by Catherine Gray (Houghton Mifflin, 1988)

 Visit Our Web Site!

INTERNET ACTIVITY
www.sbgmath.com

© Silver Burdett Ginn Inc. All rights

Name_____

There are 3 in the yard.

There are 2 on the path.

How many  are there altogether?

 Understand
You need to find out how
many wagons in all.

 Plan
You can draw a picture.
Then write a number sentence.

I draw 3 wagons
and 2 more.

 Solve

$$\underline{3} + \underline{2} = \underline{5} \text{ wagons}$$

Look Back
How did the picture help you decide
what number sentence to write?

Draw a picture to solve.
Write the addition sentence.

1. 2 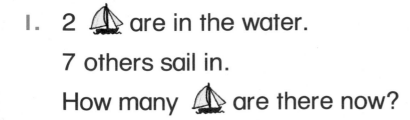 are in the water.

   7 others sail in.

   How many 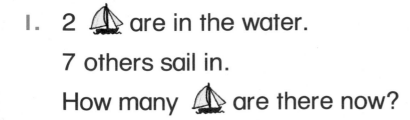 are there now?

   _____ + _____ = _____ boats

Home Connection Drawing pictures can help solve word problems.
Your child can practice this strategy by drawing pictures.

one hundred nine   **109**

Draw a picture to solve.
Write the addition sentence.

1. There is 1 big   .
   There are 3 little  .
   How many are there in all?

   _____ + _____ = _____ kites

2. Mika sees 4 big  .
   Then she sees 4 little  .
   How many does she see altogether?

   _____ + _____ = _____ boats

3. Jared has 4   .
   Cora has 2 more than Jared.
   How many  does Cora have?

   _____ + _____ = _____ wagons

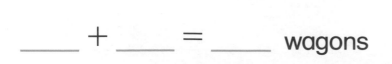

© Silver Burdett Ginn Inc. All Rights Reserved

You can count back from any number.

Start at 7.
Count back 6, 5, 4.

6 , 5 , 4

Use counters if you like.
Count back.
Write the numbers.

Word Bank
count back

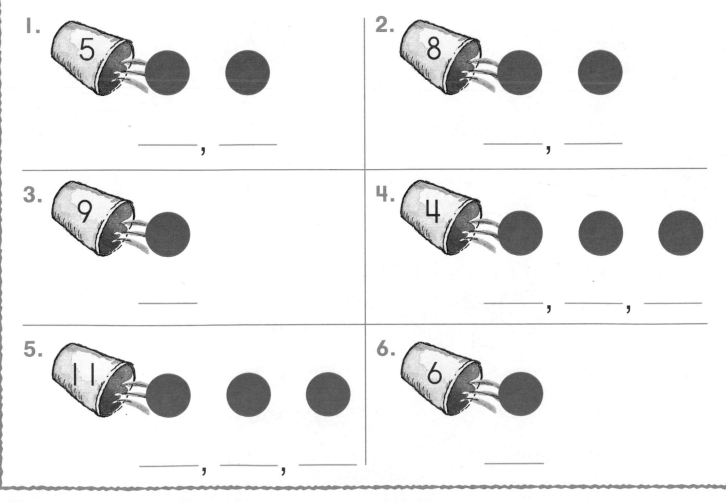

1. 5 _____ , _____

2. 8 _____ , _____

3. 9 _____

4. 4 _____ , _____ , _____

5. 11 _____ , _____ , _____

6. 6 _____

Home Connection Counting back from a number is a strategy
children can use to subtract. Use buttons or other small items to
help your child practice counting back from different numbers.

Use counters if you like.
Count back. Write the numbers.

1.

6

2.

_____ , _____ , _____

3.

_____ , _____ , _____

4.

_____ , _____

5.

_____ , _____

6.

_____

Count back to solve.

7. Sal has 10 cookies.

He eats   .

How many cookies

are left?

_____ cookies

8. What if Sal eats

  more?

Now how many

cookies will be left?

_____ cookies

© Silver Burdett Ginn Inc. All rights reserved.

| Start with 5. | Count back 2. | $5 - 2 = 3$ |

Count back to subtract.

1.

$4 - 1 = 3$

2.

$6 - 2 = 4$

3.

$7 - 1 = 6$

4.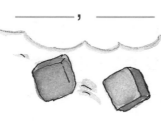

$9 - 2 = 7$

 Home Connection Your child has been counting back to find differences. Have your child use beans, pebbles, or pennies to review the subtraction problems on this page.

Count back to subtract.

1.  

$$\begin{array}{r} 8 \\ -1 \\ \hline 7 \end{array}$$

2.

$$\begin{array}{r} 5 \\ -2 \\ \hline 3 \end{array}$$

3.
$$\begin{array}{r} 6 \\ -1 \\ \hline 5 \end{array}$$
$$\begin{array}{r} 4 \\ -2 \\ \hline 2 \end{array}$$
$$\begin{array}{r} 5 \\ -1 \\ \hline 4 \end{array}$$
$$\begin{array}{r} 9 \\ -2 \\ \hline 8 \end{array}$$
$$\begin{array}{r} 2 \\ -1 \\ \hline 1 \end{array}$$
$$\begin{array}{r} 8 \\ -2 \\ \hline 6 \end{array}$$

4.
$$\begin{array}{r} 9 \\ -1 \\ \hline 8 \end{array}$$
$$\begin{array}{r} 3 \\ -2 \\ \hline 1 \end{array}$$
$$\begin{array}{r} 3 \\ -1 \\ \hline 2 \end{array}$$
$$\begin{array}{r} 4 \\ -1 \\ \hline 3 \end{array}$$
$$\begin{array}{r} 6 \\ -2 \\ \hline 4 \end{array}$$
$$\begin{array}{r} 7 \\ -2 \\ \hline 5 \end{array}$$

 Critical Thinking Corner

Number Sense Journal Idea

 When would you count on?
When would you count back?
Share your ideas.

© Silver Burdett Ginn Inc. All rights reserved.

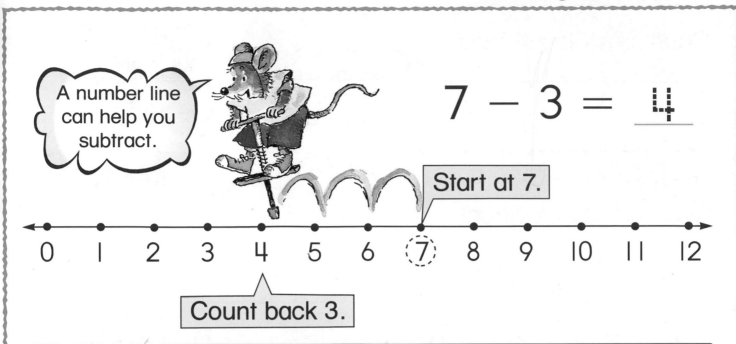

A number line can help you subtract.

$$7 - 3 = \underline{4}$$

Start at 7.

0 1 2 3 4 5 6 (7) 8 9 10 11 12

Count back 3.

Use the number line to count back.
Circle the number where you start.
Write each difference.

1.

$$8 - 3 = \underline{5}$$

0 1 2 3 4 5 6 7 (8)

2.

$$5 - 2 = \underline{3}$$

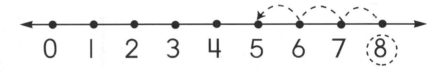

0 1 2 3 4 5 6 7 8

3.

$$4 - 3 = \underline{2}$$

0 1 2 3 4 5 6 7 8

4.

$$7 - 2 = \underline{6}$$

0 1 2 3 4 5 6 7 8

5.

$$6 - 3 = \underline{5}$$

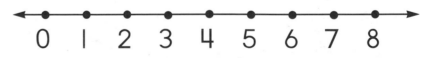

0 1 2 3 4 5 6 7 8

Home Connection A number line can be used
to count back. Ask your child to show you how he or
she used the number line to solve these problems.

Use the number line to help you.

$$\leftarrow\!\!\bullet\!\!-\!\!\bullet\!\!-\!\!\bullet\!\!-\!\!\bullet\!\!-\!\!\bullet\!\!-\!\!\bullet\!\!-\!\!\bullet\!\!-\!\!\bullet\!\!-\!\!\bullet\!\!-\!\!\bullet\!\!-\!\!\bullet\!\!-\!\!\bullet\!\!-\!\!\bullet\!\!\rightarrow$$

0 1 2 3 4 5 6 7 8 9 10 11 12

Count back to subtract.

1. $10 - 3 = \underline{7}$ $6 - 2 = \underline{8}$ $10 - 1 = \underline{9}$

2. $8 - 2 = \underline{7}$ $9 - 2 = \underline{8}$ $11 - 2 = \underline{10}$

3.
$$\begin{array}{cccccc} 6 & 7 & 8 & 10 & 4 & 6 \\ \underline{-1} & \underline{-3} & \underline{-1} & \underline{-2} & \underline{-2} & \underline{-3} \\ 5 & & & & & \end{array}$$

4.
$$\begin{array}{cccccc} 2 & 5 & 9 & 7 & 7 & 3 \\ \underline{-1} & \underline{-2} & \underline{-1} & \underline{-2} & \underline{-1} & \underline{-2} \\ 0 & 4 & & & & \end{array}$$

PROBLEM SOLVING

Problem Solving

Solve.

5. Earl has 12 big kites and 3 little kites. How many more big kites does he have?

_____ big kites

6. What if Earl buys 2 more little kites? How many little kites will he have?

_____ little kites

© Silver Burdett Ginn Inc. All rights reserved.

Doubles can help you subtract!

$2 + 2 = 4$

so $4 - 2 = 2$

$2 + 2 = \underline{4}$

$4 - 2 = \underline{2}$

Add the double and then subtract.
Use cubes if you like.

1.

$3 + 3 = \underline{}$

so $6 - 3 = \underline{}$

2.

$5 + 5 = \underline{}$

so $10 - 5 = \underline{}$

3.

$6 + 6 = \underline{}$

so $12 - 6 = \underline{}$

4.

$4 + 4 = \underline{}$

so $8 - 4 = \underline{}$

Home Connection Children can use their knowledge of doubles
to make subtraction easier. Have your child add a double, such
as $5 + 5 = 10$, and then subtract with five fingers ($10 - 5 = 5$).

Race down the track.
Add or subtract.

$$\begin{array}{r} 1 \\ -\ 1 \\ \hline 0 \end{array}$$

$$\begin{array}{r} 6 \\ +\ 6 \\ \hline \end{array}$$

$$\begin{array}{r} 10 \\ -\ 6 \\ \hline \end{array}$$

$$\begin{array}{r} 4 \\ +\ 4 \\ \hline \end{array}$$

$$\begin{array}{r} 12 \\ -\ 6 \\ \hline \end{array}$$

$$\begin{array}{r} 4 \\ -\ 2 \\ \hline \end{array}$$

$$\begin{array}{r} 11 \\ -\ 6 \\ \hline \end{array}$$

$$\begin{array}{r} 2 \\ -\ 1 \\ \hline \end{array}$$

$$\begin{array}{r} 3 \\ +\ 3 \\ \hline \end{array}$$

$$\begin{array}{r} 10 \\ -\ 5 \\ \hline \end{array}$$

$$\begin{array}{r} 5 \\ +\ 5 \\ \hline \end{array}$$

$$\begin{array}{r} 2 \\ +\ 2 \\ \hline \end{array}$$

$$\begin{array}{r} 1 \\ +\ 1 \\ \hline \end{array}$$

$$\begin{array}{r} 8 \\ -\ 4 \\ \hline \end{array}$$

$$\begin{array}{r} 6 \\ -\ 5 \\ \hline \end{array}$$

$$\begin{array}{r} 6 \\ -\ 3 \\ \hline \end{array}$$

What Do You Think?

Journal Idea

 When I see 10 − 5, I think of a double.
Tell how you use doubles to subtract.

| **Word Bank** |
| fact family |

$5 + 4 = 9$ $9 - 4 = 5$

$4 + 5 = 9$ $9 - 5 = 4$

Write each fact family.
Use cubes if you like.

1.

___ + ___ = ___   ___ − ___ = ___

___ + ___ = ___   ___ − ___ = ___

2.

___ + ___ = ___   ___ − ___ = ___

___ + ___ = ___   ___ − ___ = ___

3.

___ + ___ = ___   ___ − ___ = ___

___ + ___ = ___   ___ − ___ = ___

Home Connection Knowing fact families can help your child add and subtract. Give your child groups of 12 or fewer objects. Have your child divide the group in two and write the fact family.

one hundred nineteen   **119**

Use the pictures.
Write each fact family.

1. 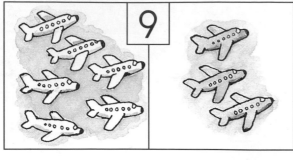 9

$$6 + 3 = 9$$

___ + ___ = ___

___ − ___ = ___

___ − ___ = ___

2.  6

___ + ___ = ___

___ + ___ = ___

___ − ___ = ___

___ − ___ = ___

3.  8

___ + ___ = ___

___ + ___ = ___

___ − ___ = ___

___ − ___ = ___

4.  7

___ + ___ = ___

___ + ___ = ___

___ − ___ = ___

___ − ___ = ___

© Silver Burdett Ginn Inc. All rights reserved.

Name_____

Add the double and then subtract.

1.  $3 + 3 =$ ____
   $6 - 3 =$ ____

2. $2 + 2 =$ ____
   $4 - 2 =$ ____

Count back to subtract.

3.
$$\begin{array}{r} 6 \\ -\ 1 \\ \hline \end{array} \qquad \begin{array}{r} 10 \\ -\ 2 \\ \hline \end{array} \qquad \begin{array}{r} 5 \\ -\ 3 \\ \hline \end{array} \qquad \begin{array}{r} 7 \\ -\ 1 \\ \hline \end{array} \qquad \begin{array}{r} 9 \\ -\ 2 \\ \hline \end{array} \qquad \begin{array}{r} 12 \\ -\ 3 \\ \hline \end{array}$$

Write the fact family.

4. ____ $+$ ____ $=$ ____   ____ $-$ ____ $=$ ____

   ____ $+$ ____ $=$ ____   ____ $-$ ____ $=$ ____

Draw a picture to solve.
Write the addition sentence.

5. There are 2 big .

   There are 5 little .

   How many are there in all?

   ____ $+$ ____ $=$ ____

Name_____ **Extra Practice**

Find each sum and difference.
Color.

4  red   5 blue   6 yellow   7 green

$$\begin{array}{r} 2 \\ + 3 \\ \hline \end{array}$$

$$\begin{array}{r} 11 \\ - 4 \\ \hline \end{array}$$

$$\begin{array}{r} 4 \\ + 2 \\ \hline \end{array}$$

$$\begin{array}{r} 10 \\ - 6 \\ \hline \end{array}$$

$$\begin{array}{r} 3 \\ + 4 \\ \hline \end{array}$$

$$\begin{array}{r} 5 \\ + 0 \\ \hline \end{array}$$

$$\begin{array}{r} 3 \\ + 1 \\ \hline \end{array}$$

$$\begin{array}{r} 11 \\ - 5 \\ \hline \end{array}$$

$$\begin{array}{r} 12 \\ - 8 \\ \hline \end{array}$$

$$\begin{array}{r} 10 \\ - 4 \\ \hline \end{array}$$

$$\begin{array}{r} 1 \\ + 6 \\ \hline \end{array}$$

$$\begin{array}{r} 12 \\ - 7 \\ \hline \end{array}$$

124   one hundred twenty-four

1. Count back to subtract.

_____ , _____

$6 - 2 = 5$

Add the doubles and then subtract.

2. $4 + 4 = 8$

$8 - 4 = 7$

3. $3 + 3 = 6$

$6 - 3 = 5$

Write the fact family.

4. $8 + 1 = 9$ ___ − ___ = ___

___ + ___ = ___   ___ − ___ = ___

Add or subtract.

5.
$$\begin{array}{cccccc} 7 & 6 & 8 & 9 & 3 & 5 \\ -3 & +4 & +3 & -6 & +2 & -3 \end{array}$$

Complete the number sentence.

6. There are 6 .

Joe buys 2 more.

How many are there now?

$6 \oplus 2 = 8$

What You Need

Spinner 1   Spinner 2

1 Spin Spinner 1.
Record the number.

2 Spin Spinner 2.
Record the number.

3 Write a number sentence and solve.

4 Tell how you found each answer.

	Spinner 1	Spinner 2	Number Sentence
1.			____ + ____ = ____
2.			____ + ____ = ____
3.			____ − ____ = ____
4.			____ + ____ = ____
5.			____ − ____ = ____

For Your Portfolio
You might put this page in your portfolio.

Name

You can count up
to subtract 10 − 7.

3

Start with 7.
Count up to 10.

7 , _8_ , _9_ , _10_

10 − 7 = _3_

Count up to subtract.
Use counters if you like.

1. 8 − 5 = (?)

Start with 5.
Count up to 8.

5, ____, ____, ____

8 − 5 = ____

2. 10 − 8 = (?)

Start with 8.
Count up to 10.

8, ____, ____

10 − 8 = ____

---

3. 12 − 9 = (?)

Start with 9.
Count up to 12.

9, ____, ____, ____

12 − 9 = ____

4. 9 − 7 = (?)

Start with 7.
Count up to 9.

7, ____, ____

9 − 7 = ____

Name_____

You can use a  to count on.

Press `ON/C` each time you begin.

Press the keys.

Write the numbers you see.

1. Count on 1.

5 + 1 = *6* = *7* = *8*

8 + 1 = *9* = ___ = ___

2. Count on 2.

3 + 2 = ___ = ___ = ___

6 + 2 = ___ = ___ = ___

3. Count on 3.

3 + 3 = ___ = ___ = ___

2 + 3 = ___ = ___ = ___

Journal Idea

 How could you use a  to count back?

Fill in the ⬭ for the correct answer.

How many are there?

1.

⬭ 10   ⬭ 8   ⬭ 12   ⬛ 11

2.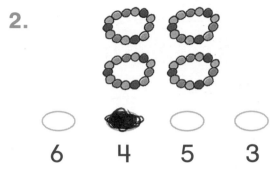

⬭ 6   ⬛ 4   ⬭ 5   ⬭ 3

What number is missing?

3. ____, 10, 11

⬭ 7   ⬛ 9   ⬭ 11   ⬭ 8

4. 7, ____, 9

⬭ 9   ⬭ 7   ⬭ 8   ⬭ 10

Add or subtract.

5. 6 + 2 = ____

⬭ 5   ⬭ 6   ⬭ 4   ⬛ 8

6. 2 + 3 = ____

⬭ 1   ⬛ 5   ⬭ 4   ⬭ 6

---

7. 8
   + 0
   _____

⬭ 0
⬛ 8
⬭ 9
⬭ 7

8. 8
   − 6
   _____

⬭ 4
⬭ 8
⬛ 2
⬭ 1

9. 5
   − 5
   _____

⬭ 1
⬭ 5
⬛ 0
⬭ 4

---

10. 6
    + 6
    _____

⬭ 10
⬭ 11
⬛ 12
⬭ 0

11. 12
    − 6
    _____

⬭ 12
⬛ 0
⬭ 5
⬛ 6

12. 10
    − 4
    _____

⬛ 6
⬭ 10
⬭ 4
⬭ 5

Chapter 4 Cumulative Review

What other fact is in the same family?

13. $4 + 4 = 8$

    ○ $4 + 0 = 4$
    ○ $8 - 4 = 4$
    ○ $12 - 8 = 4$
    ○ $8 + 2 = 10$

14. $6 - 1 = 5$

    ○ $6 - 5 = 1$
    ○ $11 - 5 = 6$
    ○ $5 - 1 = 4$
    ○ $6 + 1 = 7$

15. $6 + 3 = 9$

    ○ $6 - 3 = 3$
    ○ $10 - 3 = 7$
    ○ $3 + 6 = 9$
    ○ $4 + 6 = 10$

16. $7 - 2 = 5$

    ○ $7 + 2 = 9$
    ○ $5 + 2 = 7$
    ○ $12 - 7 = 5$
    ○ $7 - 6 = 1$

Choose the correct number sentence.

17.

    ○ $1 + 3 = 4$
    ○ $4 + 1 = 5$
    ○ $4 + 2 = 6$

18.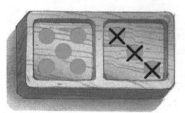

    ○ $8 - 3 = 5$
    ○ $5 - 3 = 2$
    ○ $8 - 0 = 8$

Solve.

19. Pete sees 10 .
    Then 8 drive away.
    Now how many
    does Pete see?

    ○ $8 + 2 = 10$
    ○ $10 - 2 = 8$
    ○ $10 - 8 = 2$

20. The team has 7 .
    They buy 4 more.
    Now how many
    do they have?

    ○ $7 + 4 = 11$
    ○ $7 - 3 = 4$
    ○ $11 - 7 = 4$

© Silver Burdett Ginn Inc. All rights reserved.

CHAPTER 5

Geometry and Fractions

Stitching Stories

written by Roscoe Murphy
illustrated by Pauline Howard

This Math Storybook belongs to

____

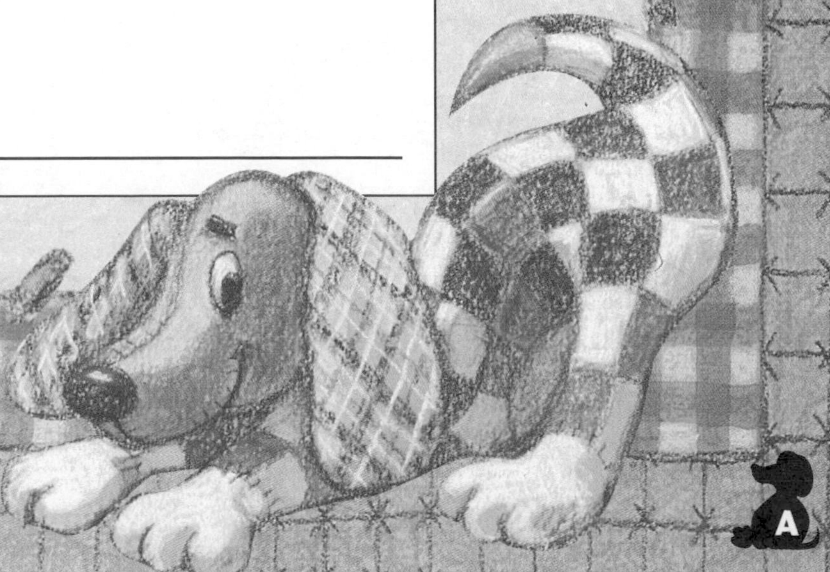

A

Today is a special day.
Matt and his mom are making a quilt.
Matt cuts out the squares.
His mom sews them together.

© Silver Burdett Ginn Inc. All rights reserved.

Matt's mom sews pictures on some squares.
Then she tells Matt stories about them.
The stories are about Matt's family.

"This square has 2 equal parts.
One part shows my old teddy bear.
One part shows me as a little girl."

© Silver Burdett Ginn Inc. All rights reserved.

"This square has a circle in it.
The circle is a wedding ring.
One half shows a picture of me.
The other half shows a picture of Dad."

"This square has 3 equal parts.
One part shows a toy.
One part shows a cradle.
The last part shows you as a baby."

© Silver Burdett Ginn Inc. All rights reserved

Here is one quilt square.
Draw something special.
Tell about the shapes you used.

INTERNET ACTIVITY
www.sbgmath.com

A Note to the Family

Here are some learning ideas you can share with your child.

Enjoy *Stitching Stories* Together

- Read the story together. Talk about how a quilt can tell the story of a person's or a family's life.
- With your child, go through each page of the book to see what shapes you can find. Look for shapes within shapes, such as circles within squares, and triangles within squares. Encourage your child to trace shapes with a finger. Also point out halves, thirds, and fourths in the square designs.
- Look at the last page of the book. Talk with your child about the shapes he or she drew to decorate the quilt square.

At-Home Activities

- Look for shapes around your home or outdoors.
- Make a shape collage out of fabric scraps.
- Explore fractions at snack times and mealtimes.

Read More About It!

To read more stories about quilts, geometry, or fractions with your child, look for the following books in your local library.

- *My Grandmother's Patchwork Quilt* by Janet Bolton (Delacorte Press, 1993)
- *The Patchwork Quilt* by Valerie Flournoy (Dial Books, 1985)
- *The Quilt-Block History of Pioneer Days* by Mary Cobb (Millbrook, 1995)
- *The Shape of Things* by Dayle Ann Dodds (Candlewick Press, 1994)

Visit Our Web Site!

INTERNET ACTIVITY
www.sbgmath.com

Name_____

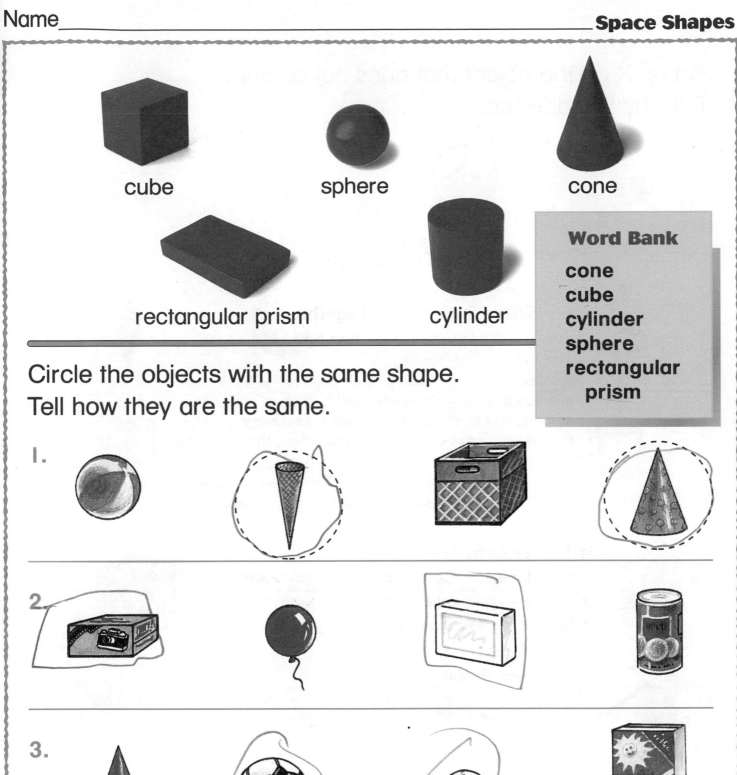

cube   sphere   cone

rectangular prism   cylinder

Word Bank

cone
cube
cylinder
sphere
rectangular
prism

Circle the objects with the same shape.
Tell how they are the same.

1.

2.

3.

4.

 Home Connection Have your child look for objects that
are shaped like cubes, cones, rectangular prisms, spheres, and
cylinders. Encourage your child to use the correct vocabulary.

Put an X on the object that does not belong.
Tell why it is different.

1.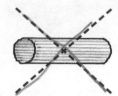

2.

3.

4.

 Critical Thinking Corner

Visual Thinking Journal Idea

 Tell how these shapes are the same.
Tell how they are different.

© Silver Burdett Ginn Inc. All rights reserved.

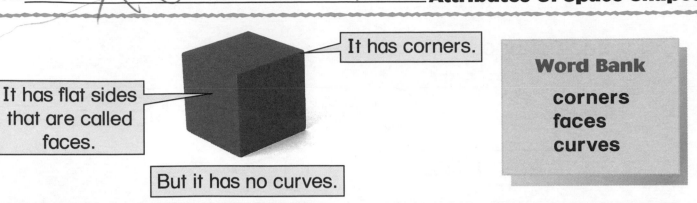

It has corners.

It has flat sides that are called faces.

But it has no curves.

Word Bank

corners
faces
curves

Use shapes if you like.

Does the shape have corners, faces, and curves?

Write **yes** or **no** in each box.

		Corners	Faces	Curves
1.	cube	yes	yes	no
2.	sphere	no	no	yes
3.	rectangular prism	yes	yes	no
4.	cylinder	yes	yes	no
5.	cone	no	no	yes

Home Connection Give your child different household objects such as a cereal box, a funnel, and a paper-towel roll. Ask whether each shape has corners, faces, and/or curves.

one hundred thirty-one   **131**

Color each shape.

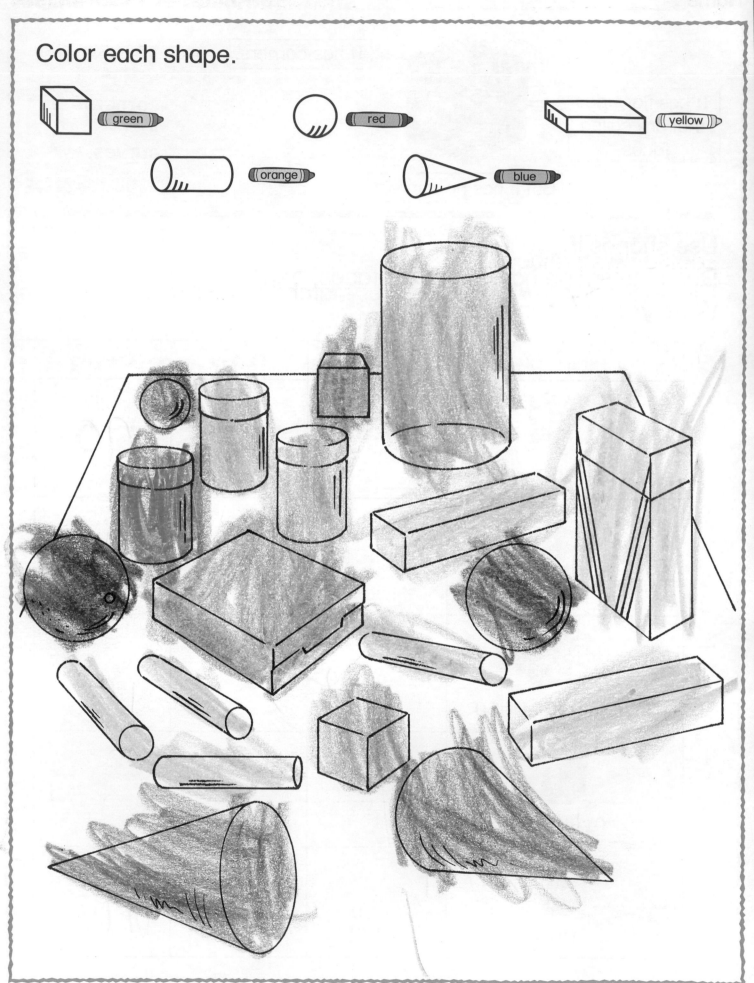

green

red

yellow

orange

blue

© Silver Burdett Ginn Inc. All rights reserved.

Look at each shape.
Circle the object with a face that matches the shape.

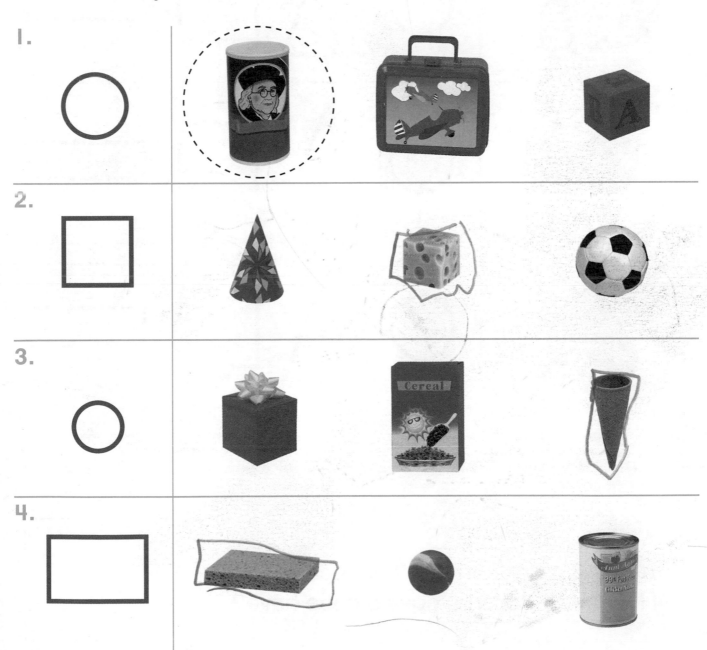

1.

2.

3.

4.

Home Connection Help your child trace on paper around the faces of household objects such as cans and boxes. Ask, "What is the shape of each tracing?"

one hundred thirty-three   **133**

Circle the shape that matches a face of each object.

1.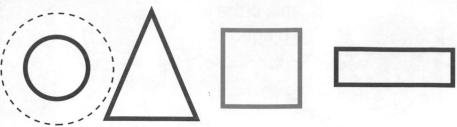

2.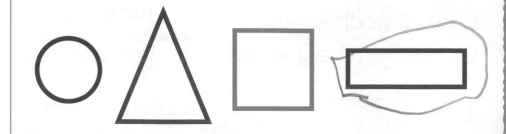

3.

4.

© Silver Burdett Ginn Inc. All rights reserved.

Problem Solving

Solve.

5. A cube has 6 faces.
   It has 2 more corners than faces.
   How many corners does a cube have?

   ___8___ corners

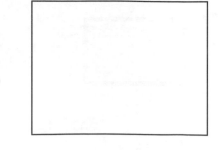

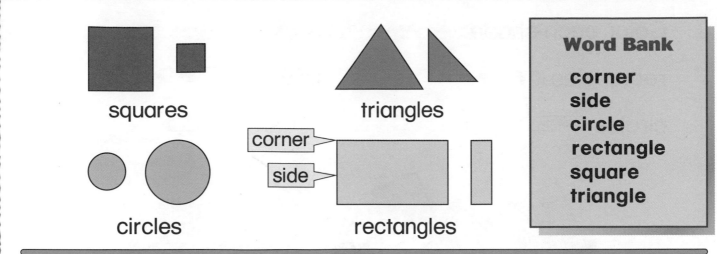

squares   triangles

corner
side

circles   rectangles

Word Bank

corner
side
circle
rectangle
square
triangle

Write how many.

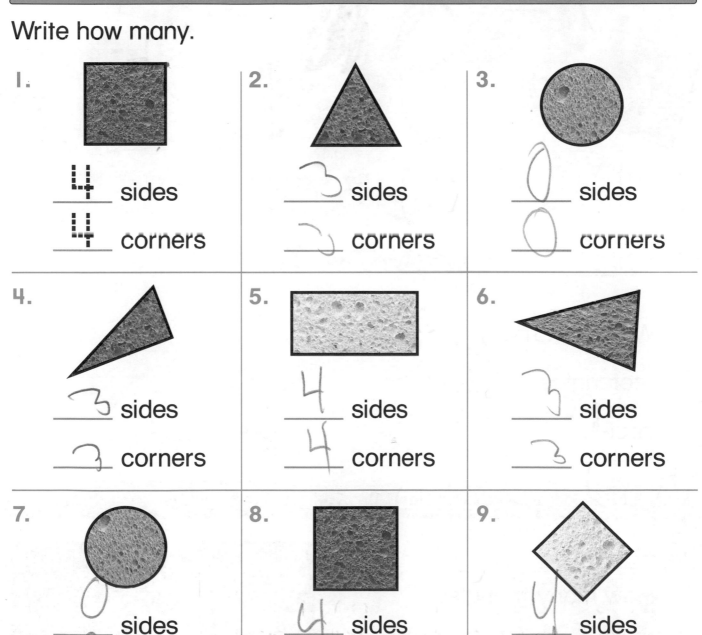

1. __4__ sides
   __4__ corners

2. __3__ sides
   __3__ corners

3. __0__ sides
   __0__ corners

4. __3__ sides
   __3__ corners

5. __4__ sides
   __4__ corners

6. __3__ sides
   __3__ corners

7. __0__ sides
   ___ corners

8. __4__ sides
   __4__ corners

9. __4__ sides
   __4__ corners

Home Connection During a walk, help your child identify shapes on street signs, houses, and stores.

one hundred thirty-five   **135**

1. Color each shape.

rectangles (green) triangles (blue)

circles (yellow) squares (red)

2. Write how many.

rectangles ____ triangles ____

circles ____ squares ____

  Critical Thinking Corner

Visual Thinking

3. How many triangles are there? ____

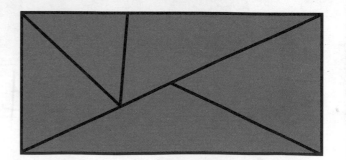

© Silver Burdett Ginn Inc. All rights reserved.

open figures   closed figures

Put an X on each open figure.
Color inside each closed figure.

Word Bank

open figure
closed figure

Home Connection Use a shoelace to create
open and closed figures for your child to identify.

one hundred thirty-seven   **137**

1. Put an X inside each closed figure.

2. Put an X on each open figure.

3. Put an X outside each closed figure.

Problem Solving

4. Make each figure closed.

Name_____ **Geometric Patterns**

What patterns do you see?

Look for a pattern.
Draw and color to show what comes next.

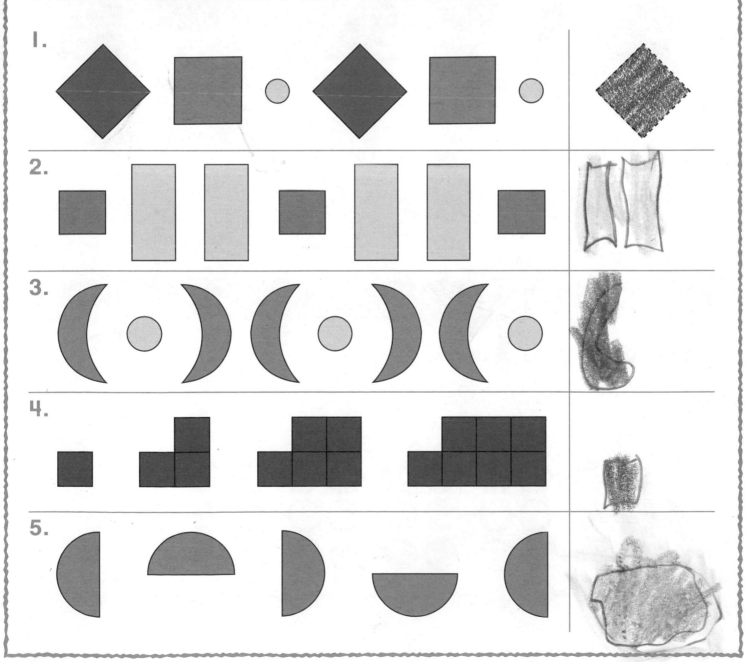

Home Connection With your child, search your
home for repeating patterns on floor tiles, wallpaper, and
furniture. Encourage your child to describe each pattern.

one hundred thirty-nine   **139**

Draw and color to complete the pattern.

1.
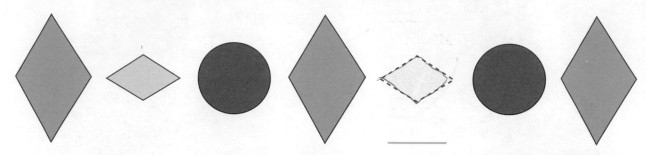

2.
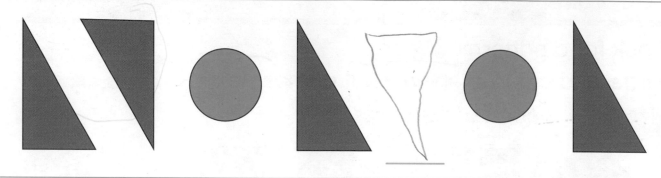

3.
  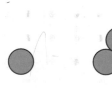   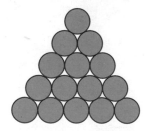

Critical Thinking Corner

Visual Thinking **Journal Idea**

What went wrong?
Tell how to fix the pattern.

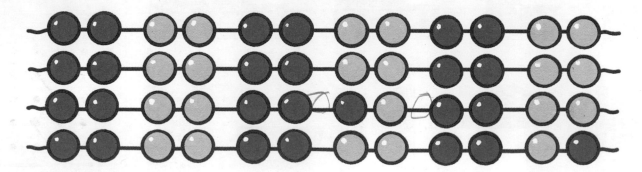

These triangles are the same size and the same shape.

Draw a shape that matches.

1.
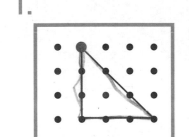 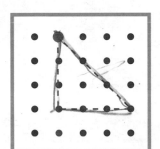

2.
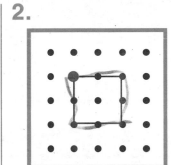 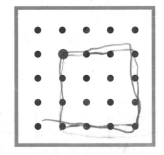

3.
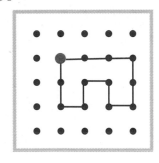 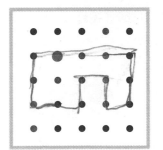

4.
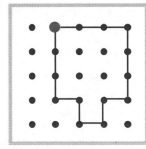 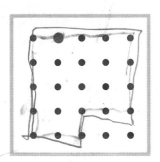

5.
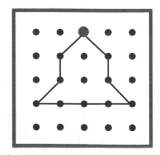 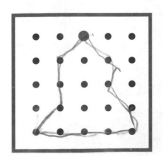

6.
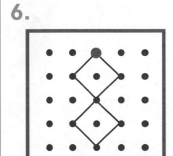 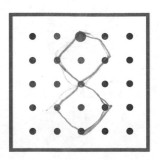

Home Connection Your child is learning to identify shapes that match in size and shape. Help your child find things around the house that are the same size and shape.

Circle the shapes that match.

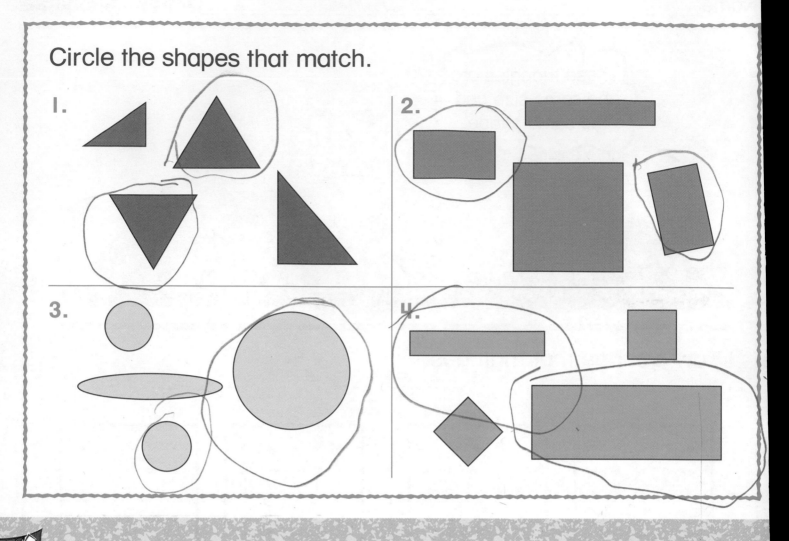

1.

2.

3.

4.

Checkpoint

1. Put an X on the object that does not belong.

   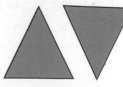

2. Color inside the closed figures.

3. Draw and color the missing shape.

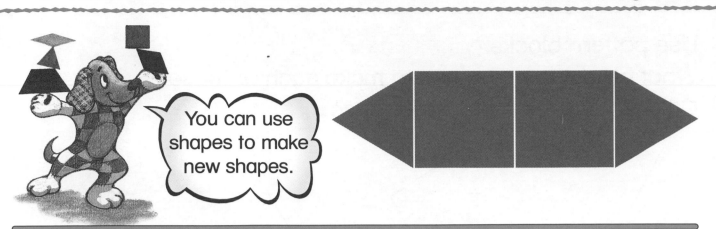

You can use shapes to make new shapes.

Use pattern blocks.

What blocks can you use to make each of these?

Color to show the blocks you use.

1.

2.

3.

4.

5.

6.

Home Connection Your child has been combining shapes to make new shapes. Look for shapes within shapes around your home and have your child tell you the shapes he or she sees.

one hundred forty-three **143**

Use pattern blocks.
What blocks can you use to make each of these?
Color to show the blocks you use.

1.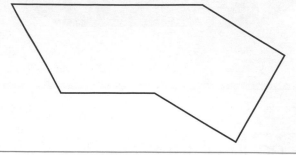

2.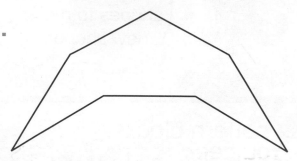

3. Make your own shape with blocks.
Trace around it.
Have a friend find which blocks you used.

Make Your Own

Problem Solving

Use pattern blocks to make this shape 3 ways.
Color to show each way.

4.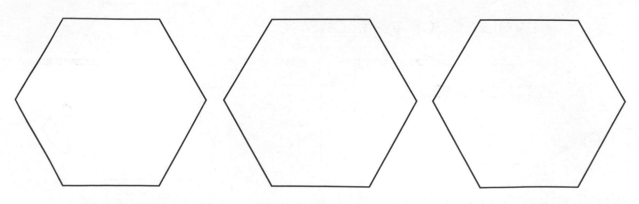

© Silver Burdett Ginn Inc. All rights reserved.

Problem Solving
Use Logical Reasoning

STRATEGY
Understand
Plan
Solve
Look Back

Name_____

Which of these shapes do you have?

My shape has 4 corners. All the sides are the same.

 Understand

You need to find the mystery shape.

 Plan

You can follow the clues.
Cross out what does not belong.

The square must be the mystery shape.

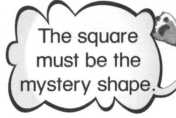

 Solve

Clue 1:
My shape has 4 corners.

Clue 2:
All the sides are the same.

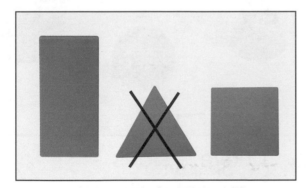 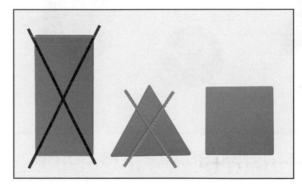

 Look Back

How can you check your answer?

Circle the correct shape.

1. I have curves.
I have faces.
What shape am I?

 Home Connection Ask your child to create a shape riddle, like the ones on this page, for you to solve.

Circle the correct shape.

1. I have sides.
   I do not have 4 corners.
   What shape am I?

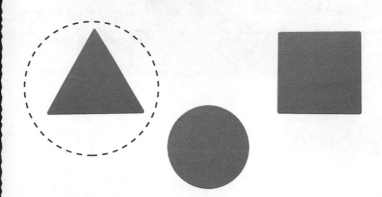

2. I have 0 sides.
   I have 0 corners.
   What shape am I?

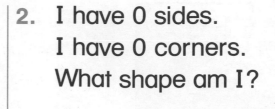

3. I have curves.
   I have 1 face.
   What shape am I?

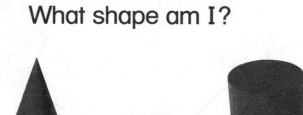

4. I have curves.
   I do not have a face.
   What shape am I?

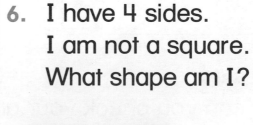

5. All my sides are the same.
   I have 3 corners.
   What shape am I?

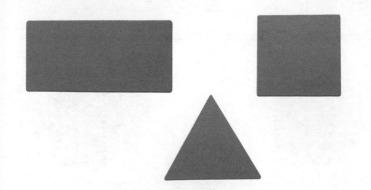

6. I have 4 sides.
   I am not a square.
   What shape am I?

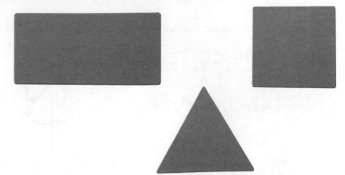

© Silver Burdett Ginn Inc. All rights reserved.

Both parts match.

Do both parts match?

Circle the objects with matching parts.

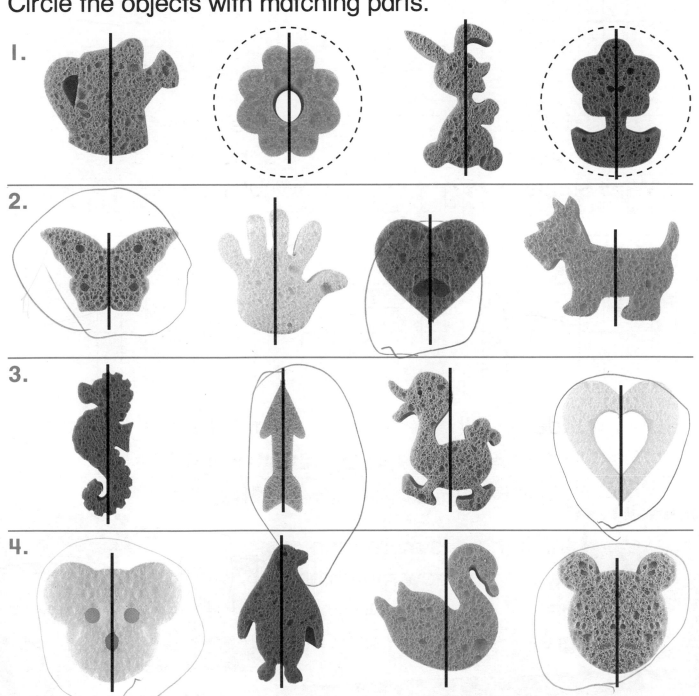

1.

2.

3.

4.

Home Connection Your child is learning to recognize symmetrical objects. Have your child look at home for shapes or objects that are symmetrical.

Draw a part to match.

1.

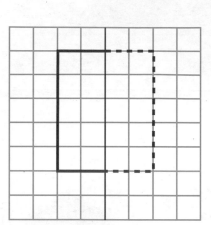

2.

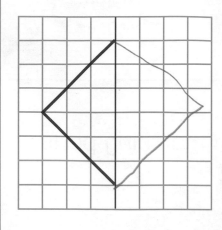

3.

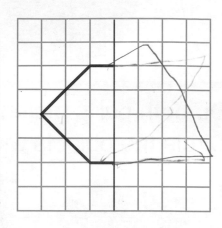

4.

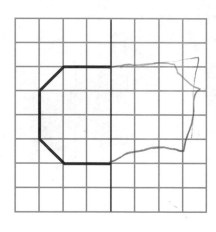

5.

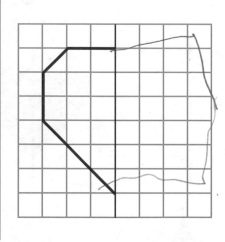

6.

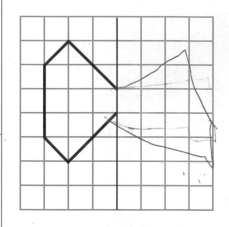

What Do You Think?

Journal Idea

I think there is more than one way to show matching parts of a square. Do you agree? Tell why or why not.

© Silver Burdett Ginn Inc. All rights reserved.

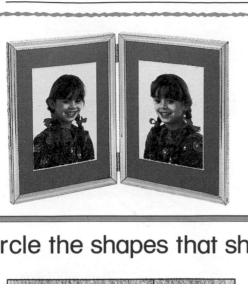

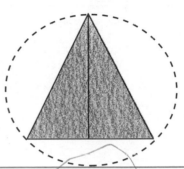

These parts are the same size and shape. The parts are equal.

Word Bank

equal parts

Circle the shapes that show equal parts.

1.

2.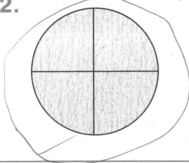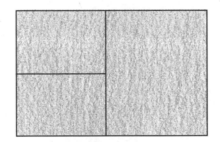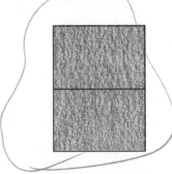

3.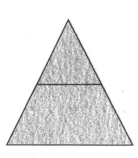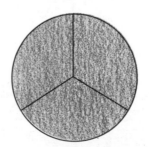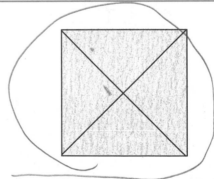

4.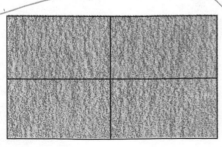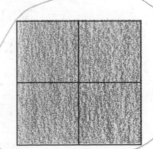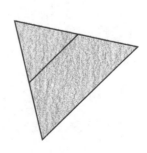

 Home Connection Recognizing equal parts helps to understand fractions. Cut out some shapes and fold them in different ways. Ask your child to tell how many equal parts are in each shape.

Write the number of equal parts.

1.
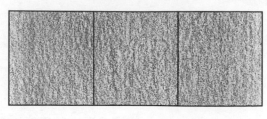

_3_

2.
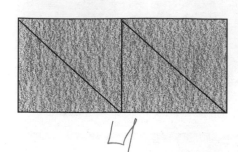

4

3.
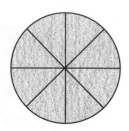

_____

4.
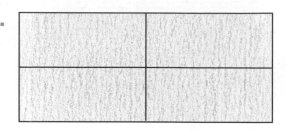

_____

5.
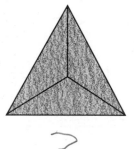

3

6.
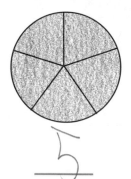

5

 **Problem Solving**

Solve.

7. Tomás wants to cut this paper into 8 equal parts. Draw lines to show where he could cut.

© Silver Burdett Ginn Inc. All rights reserved

Name_____

There are 2 equal parts.
Each part is one half
of the whole.

$\frac{1}{2}$ $\frac{1}{2}$

Word Bank

one half

Circle each shape that shows halves.

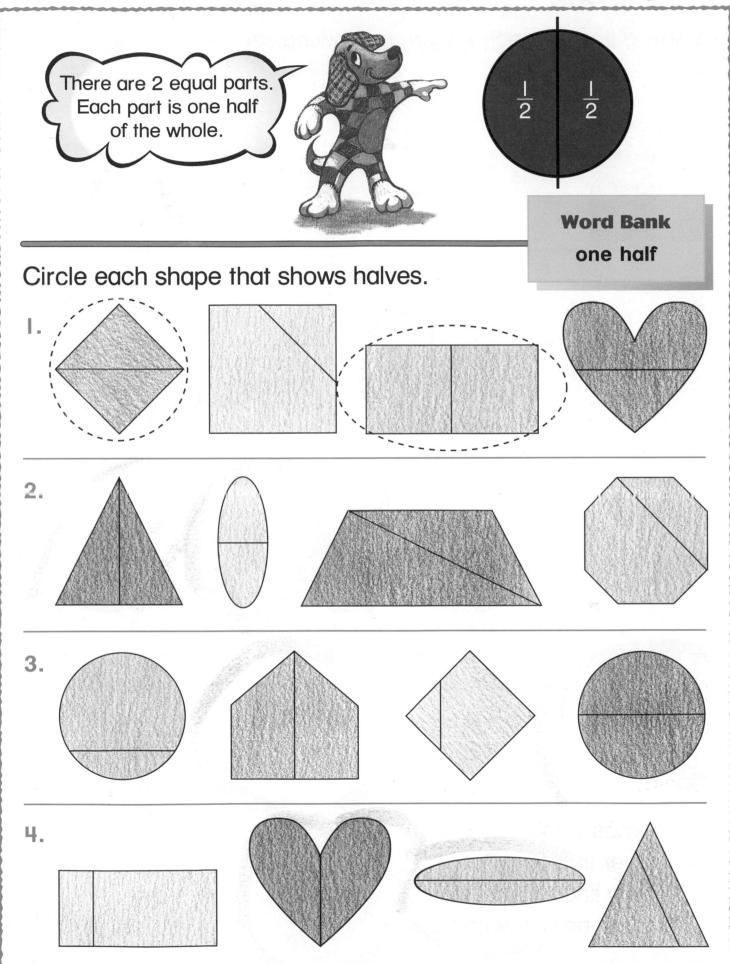

Home Connection Your child is learning to recognize
halves. Help your child cut paper shapes into two parts. Make
some parts equal. Ask your child to tell which shapes show halves.

one hundred fifty-one   **151**

Draw a line on each shape to show halves.

Color $\frac{1}{2}$ of each shape.

1.

2.

3.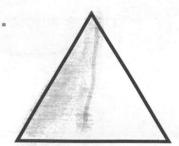

4.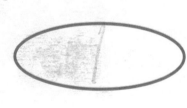

5.

6.

7.

8.

9.

Critical Thinking Corner

Number Sense   **Journal Idea**

   Andy has $\frac{1}{2}$ of a sandwich.

Eva has $\frac{1}{2}$ of a sandwich.

Eva says she has more than Andy.

Could she be right?   NO

Tell why or why not.

© Silver Burdett Ginn Inc. All rights reserved.

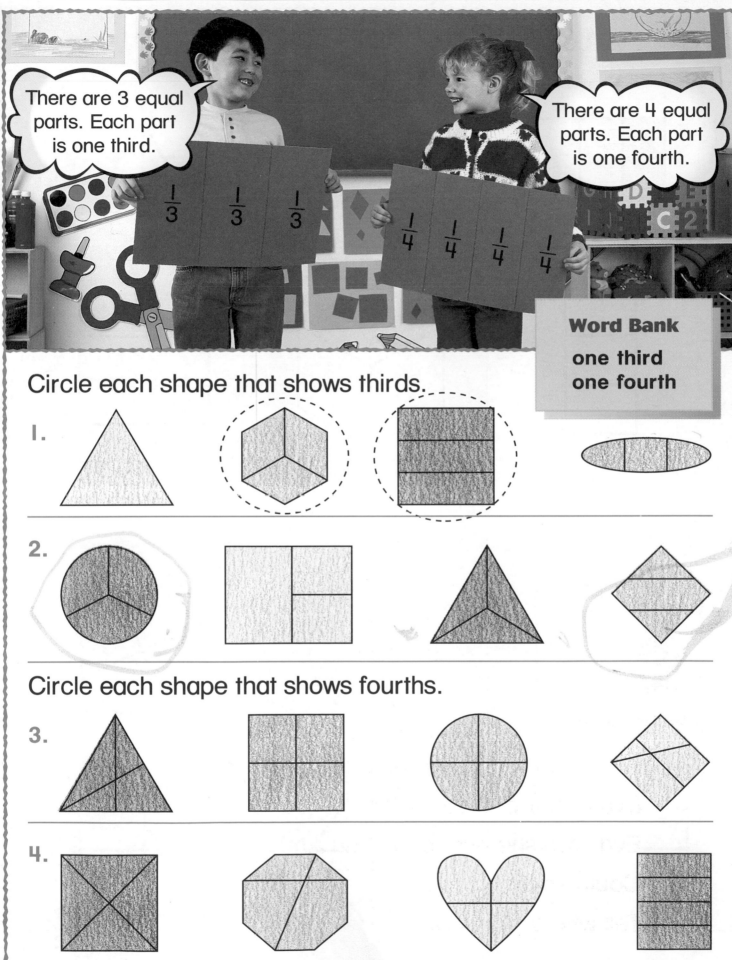

There are 3 equal parts. Each part is one third.

$\frac{1}{3}$ $\frac{1}{3}$ $\frac{1}{3}$

There are 4 equal parts. Each part is one fourth.

$\frac{1}{4}$ $\frac{1}{4}$ $\frac{1}{4}$ $\frac{1}{4}$

Word Bank
one third
one fourth

Circle each shape that shows thirds.

1.

2.

Circle each shape that shows fourths.

3.

4.

Home Connection Help your child make paper shapes and then fold or cut them to show thirds and fourths.

one hundred fifty-three **153**

Color $\frac{1}{3}$ of each shape.

1.
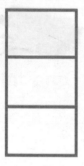

2.

3.
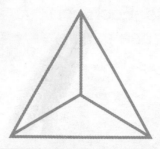

4.

5.

6.

Color $\frac{1}{4}$ of each shape.

7.
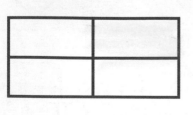

8.
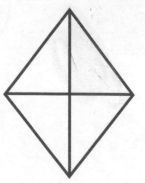

9.
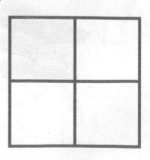

10.
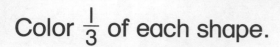

11.

12.

© Silver Burdett Ginn Inc. All rights reserved.

Name_____ **Fractions of a Group**

$\frac{1}{3}$ is blue.

There are 3 pompoms.
One is blue.
One third of the group
is blue.

What part is blue?
Circle the fraction.

1.

$\frac{1}{2}$ $\frac{1}{3}$ $\left(\frac{1}{4}\right)$

2.

$\frac{1}{2}$ $\frac{1}{3}$ $\frac{1}{4}$

3.

$\frac{1}{2}$ $\frac{1}{3}$ $\frac{1}{4}$

4.

$\frac{1}{2}$ $\frac{1}{3}$ $\frac{1}{4}$

5.

$\frac{1}{2}$ $\frac{1}{3}$ $\frac{1}{4}$

6.

$\frac{1}{2}$ $\frac{1}{3}$ $\frac{1}{4}$

 Home Connection Your child is learning to identify
fractions of a group. Show your child 2, 3, or 4 identical
objects. Have your child identify $\frac{1}{2}$, $\frac{1}{3}$, or $\frac{1}{4}$ of them.

one hundred fifty-five **155**

Color to show each fraction.

1. $\frac{1}{3}$

2. $\frac{1}{2}$

3. $\frac{1}{4}$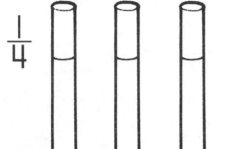

4. $\frac{1}{3}$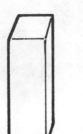

5. $\frac{1}{4}$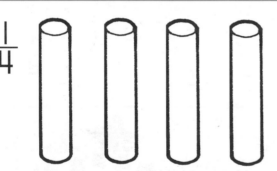

6. $\frac{1}{2}$

Problem Solving

Journal Idea

 Solve.

Mike has $\frac{1}{3}$ of a jar of paint.

Lee has $\frac{1}{4}$ of a jar of paint.

The jars are the same size.

Who has more paint? _____

Tell how you know.

© Silver Burdett Ginn Inc. All rights reserved.

156   one hundred fifty-six

APPLICATION
Understand
Plan
Look Back
Solve

Problem Solving
Exploring Fair Shares

Name_____

We each have a fair share.

Circle each child's fair share.

Use counters if you like.

Think: A fair share means everyone gets the same amount.

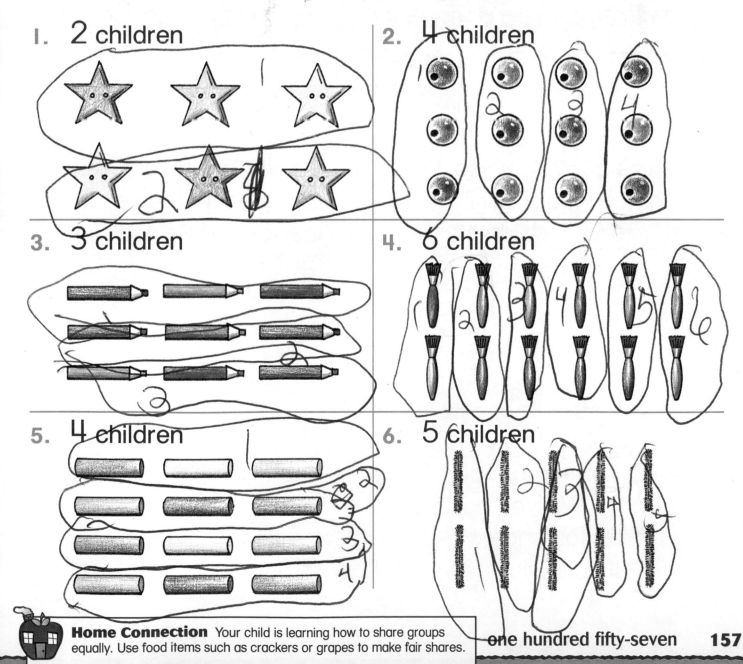

1. 2 children

2. 4 children

3. 3 children

4. 6 children

5. 4 children

6. 5 children

Home Connection Your child is learning how to share groups equally. Use food items such as crackers or grapes to make fair shares.

one hundred fifty-seven   **157**

Solve. Circle **yes** or **no**.

1. Can you make fair shares for 2 children?

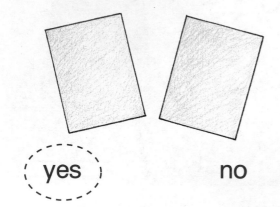

(yes)　　　　no

2. Can you make fair shares for 3 children?

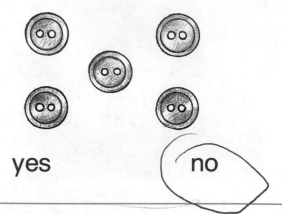

yes　　　　(no)

3. Can you make fair shares for 4 children?

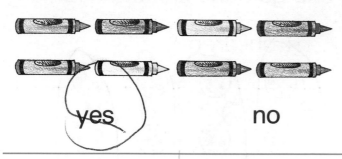

(yes)　　　　no

4. Can you make fair shares for 2 children?

(yes)　　　　no

5. There are 9 marbles. Can you make fair shares for 3 children?

yes　　　　(no)

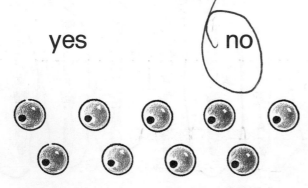

What if one more person comes? Will you be able to make fair shares?

yes　　　　no

6. Tim and Tina have a pie cut into 4 equal pieces. Can they each have a fair share?

(yes)　　　　no

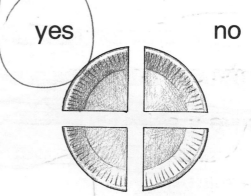

What if 2 more people come? Will they be able to make fair shares?

yes　　　　no

© Silver Burdett Ginn Inc. All rights reserved

Name_____

Draw a shape that matches.

1.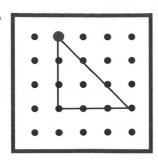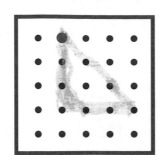

2.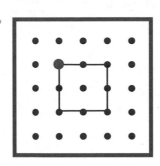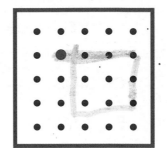

Circle the shapes that show equal parts.

3.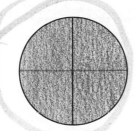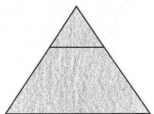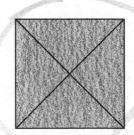

Color to show each fraction.

4. $\frac{1}{2}$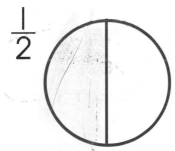

5. $\frac{1}{3}$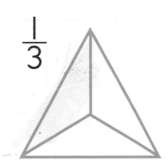

6. $\frac{1}{4}$

Circle the correct shape.

7. I have 4 sides.
   All 4 sides are the same.
   What shape am I?

8. I have curves.
   I am not a sphere.
   What shape am I?

I. Be a shape detective.
How many of each shape
do you see?

circles ————

squares ————

triangles ————

rectangles ————

2. Be a fraction detective.
Color the circles
that show each fraction.

halves   ⬱ yellow ⬱

thirds   ⬱ green ⬱

fourths   ⬱ red ⬱

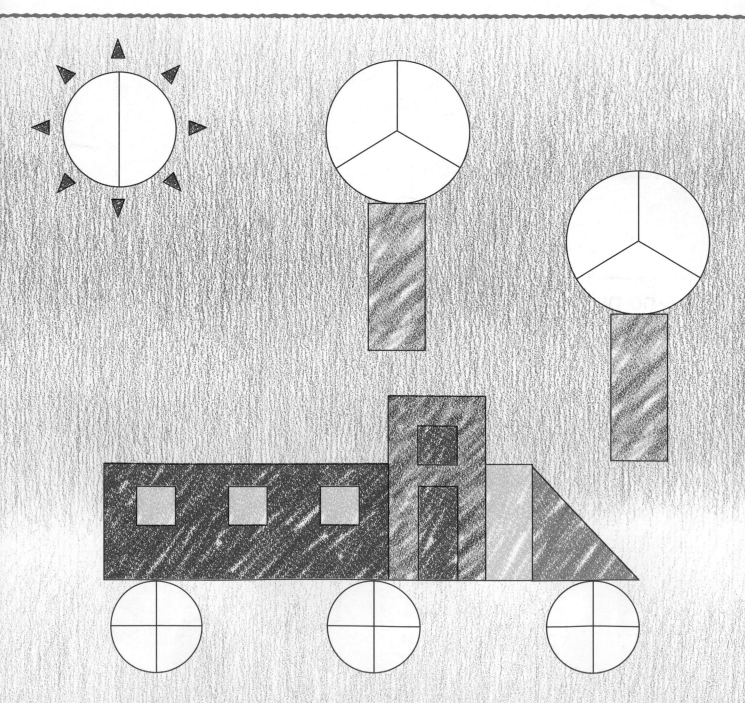

© Silver Burdett Ginn Inc. All rights reserved.

Name_____
Chapter Test

Circle the objects with the same shape.

1.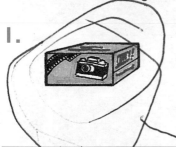

Write the number of sides and corners.

2.  $\underline{4}$ sides $\underline{4}$ corners

3.  $\underline{3}$ sides $\underline{3}$ corners

Color inside the closed figures.

4.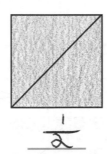

Write the number of equal parts.

5. 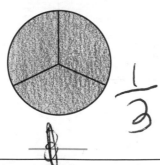 $\frac{1}{3}$ $\underline{}$

6. 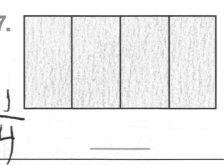 $\frac{1}{2}$ $\underline{}$

7. $\frac{1}{4}$ $\underline{}$

Circle fair shares for 4 children.

8.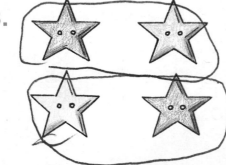

Name_____ **Performance Assessment**

What You Need

can

block

1️⃣ Trace a face of each object.

2️⃣ Look at the shape you made.

3️⃣ Write how many corners and sides.

_____ sides   _____ corners | _____ sides   _____ corners

4️⃣ Draw a line on one of the shapes to show 2 equal parts. Color $\frac{1}{2}$.

5️⃣ Draw lines on the other shape to show 4 equal parts. Color $\frac{1}{4}$.

 For Your Portfolio

You might put this page in your portfolio.

© Silver Burdett Ginn Inc. All rights reserved.

8  around

Count how many 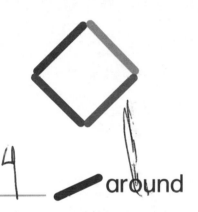 around.

1.

4 around

2.

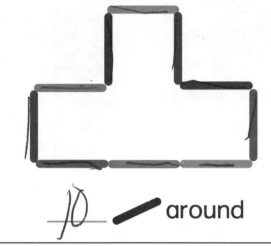

10 around

3.

3  around

4.

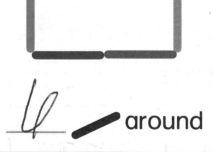

6 around

5.

6  around

6.

7  around

Name_____

You can use the MathProcessor
to show fractions.

What fraction does each strip show?

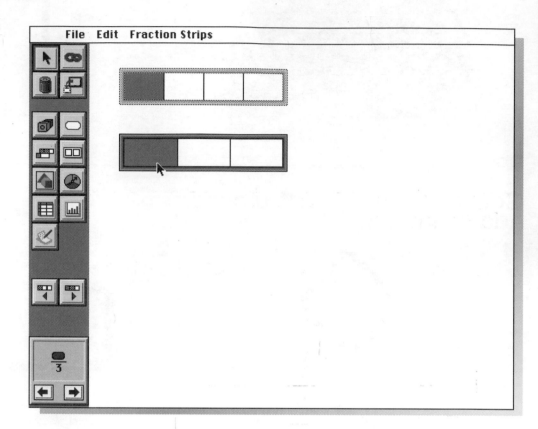

Work with a partner.

1 Click on the **fraction strip button**
to show a fraction strip.

2 Click on the **arrow** to tell how many
equal parts. Then click on the **number**.

3 Click on one part of the **fraction strip**.
What fraction did you show?

Show other fractions.
Tell about the number of equal parts.

© Silver Burdett Ginn Inc. All rights reserved.

Name_____

Fill in the  for the correct answer.

1. Which shows 8?

⬭

⬭

⬭

2. Which shows 10?

⬭

⬭

⬭

Add or subtract.

3. $6 + 1 =$ ___

⬭   ⬭   ⬭   ⬭
5   7   8   6

4. $3 + 3 =$ ___

⬭   ⬭   ⬭   ⬭
9   3   6   5

5. $7 - 5 =$ ___

⬭   ⬭   ⬭   ⬭
7   1   5   2

6. $4 - 2 =$ ___

⬭   ⬭   ⬭   ⬭
2   4   3   0

---

7. $\begin{array}{r} 8 \\ -0 \\ \hline \end{array}$
⬭ 0
⬭ 8
⬭ 7
⬭ 6

8. $\begin{array}{r} 1 \\ +9 \\ \hline \end{array}$
⬭ 12
⬭ 11
⬭ 10
⬭ 9

9. $\begin{array}{r} 6 \\ +5 \\ \hline \end{array}$
⬭ 11
⬭ 10
⬭ 12
⬭ 9

---

10. $\begin{array}{r} 8 \\ +3 \\ \hline \end{array}$
⬭ 5
⬭ 9
⬭ 11
⬭ 10

11. $\begin{array}{r} 11 \\ -3 \\ \hline \end{array}$
⬭ 7
⬭ 6
⬭ 9
⬭ 8

12. $\begin{array}{r} 12 \\ -8 \\ \hline \end{array}$
⬭ 6
⬭ 2
⬭ 4
⬭ 3

What other fact is in the same family?

13. $5 + 4 = 9$

- ⬭ $5 - 4 = 1$
- 🖊 $4 + 5 = 9$
- ⬭ $9 - 6 = 3$
- ⬭ $9 + 4 = 13$

14. $8 - 7 = 1$

- ⬭ $8 + 1 = 9$
- ⬭ $7 - 4 = 3$
- ⬭ $7 + 1 = 8$
- ⬭ $4 + 3 = 7$

Which object has the same shape?

15.

16.

What part is red?

17.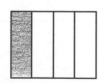

⬭   ⬭   🖊

$\dfrac{1}{2}$ $\dfrac{1}{3}$ $\dfrac{1}{4}$

18.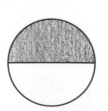

🖊   ⬭   ⬭

$\dfrac{1}{2}$ $\dfrac{1}{3}$ $\dfrac{1}{4}$

19.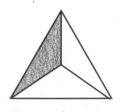

⬭   🖊   ⬭

$\dfrac{1}{2}$ $\dfrac{1}{3}$ $\dfrac{1}{4}$

Solve.

20. I have faces.
I have corners.
What shape am I?

⬭   ⬭   ⬭

Name_____ **Patterns and Numbers to 19**

Use ▭▭▭▭, ▪, and Workmat 5.
Build and write each number.

Word Bank
tens
ones

1. I ten 0 ones ___10___   ten

2. I ten I one ___⬜___   eleven

3. I ten 2 ones _____   twelve

4. I ten 3 ones _____   thirteen

5. I ten 4 ones _____   fourteen

6. I ten 5 ones _____   fifteen

7. I ten 6 ones _____   sixteen

8. I ten 7 ones _____   seventeen

9. I ten 8 ones _____   eighteen

10. I ten 9 ones _____   nineteen

Home Connection Your child is learning to show any
number from 11–19 as one ten and some ones. Have your
child use small objects to show the numbers on this page.

one hundred sixty-five **165**

Write how many.

1.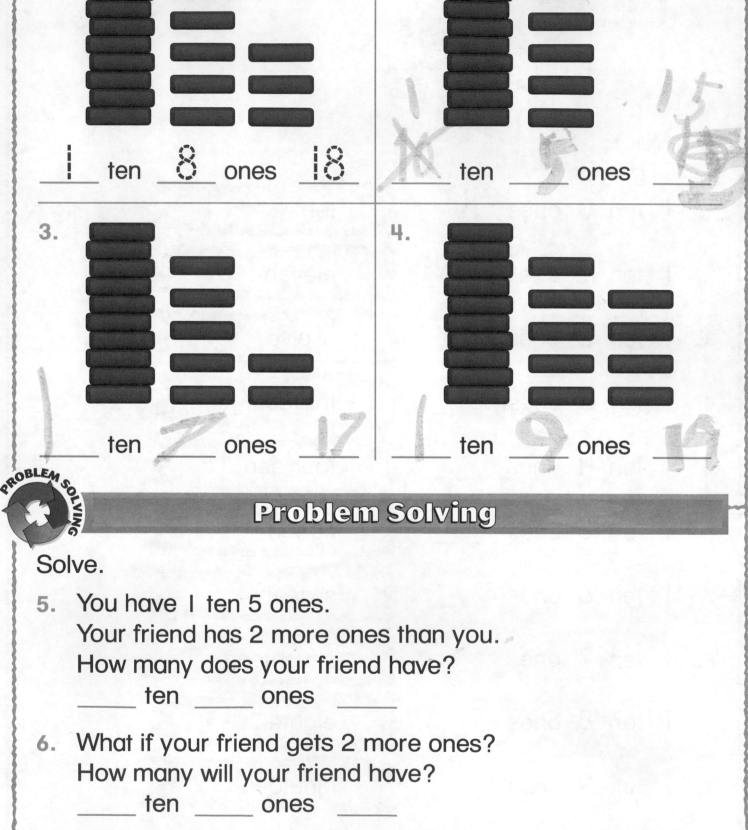

_1_ ten _8_ ones _18_

2. _____ ten _5_ ones _____

3. _____ ten _2_ ones _17_

4. _1_ ten _9_ ones _____

© Silver Burdett Ginn Inc. All rights reserved.

Problem Solving

Solve.

5. You have 1 ten 5 ones.
   Your friend has 2 more ones than you.
   How many does your friend have?
   _____ ten _____ ones _____

6. What if your friend gets 2 more ones?
   How many will your friend have?
   _____ ten _____ ones _____

__1__ group of ten = __10__

10 ones
equal 1 ten.

Circle groups of ten. Write how many.

1.

_____ groups of ten = _____

2.

_____ groups of ten = _____

3.

_____ groups of ten = _____

4.

_____ groups of ten = _____

Home Connection Have your child make groups of ten at home, using toys, coins, or crayons. Help your child count to see how many he or she has in all.

one hundred sixty-seven   **167**

Guess how many. Then circle tens and count.

1.
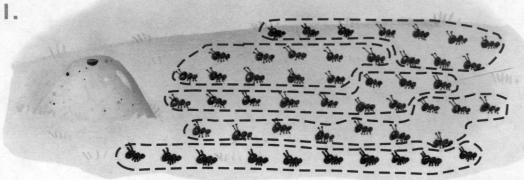

Guess
40

Count
50

2.

Guess
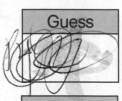

Count
20

3.

Guess
5b

Count
2b

What Do You Think?

Estimation Journal Idea

 I think seeing 10 helps me
estimate the total.
Do you agree? Tell why or why not.

© Silver Burdett Ginn Inc. All rights reserved.

Name_____

THERE'S ALWAYS A WAY!

How can you show 33?

33

3 tens 3 ones

Use , , and Workmat 5.
Build and write each number.

1.	7 tens	6 ones		2.	1 ten	9 ones
		76				19
3.	4 tens	0 ones		4.	5 tens	8 ones
		40				58
5.	8 tens	3 ones		6.	3 tens	5 ones
		83				35
7.	9 tens	6 ones		8.	2 tens	3 ones
		96				23

Home Connection Ask your child to use numbers or words to express two-digit numbers in ways illustrated on this page.

one hundred seventy-five   **175**

Match.

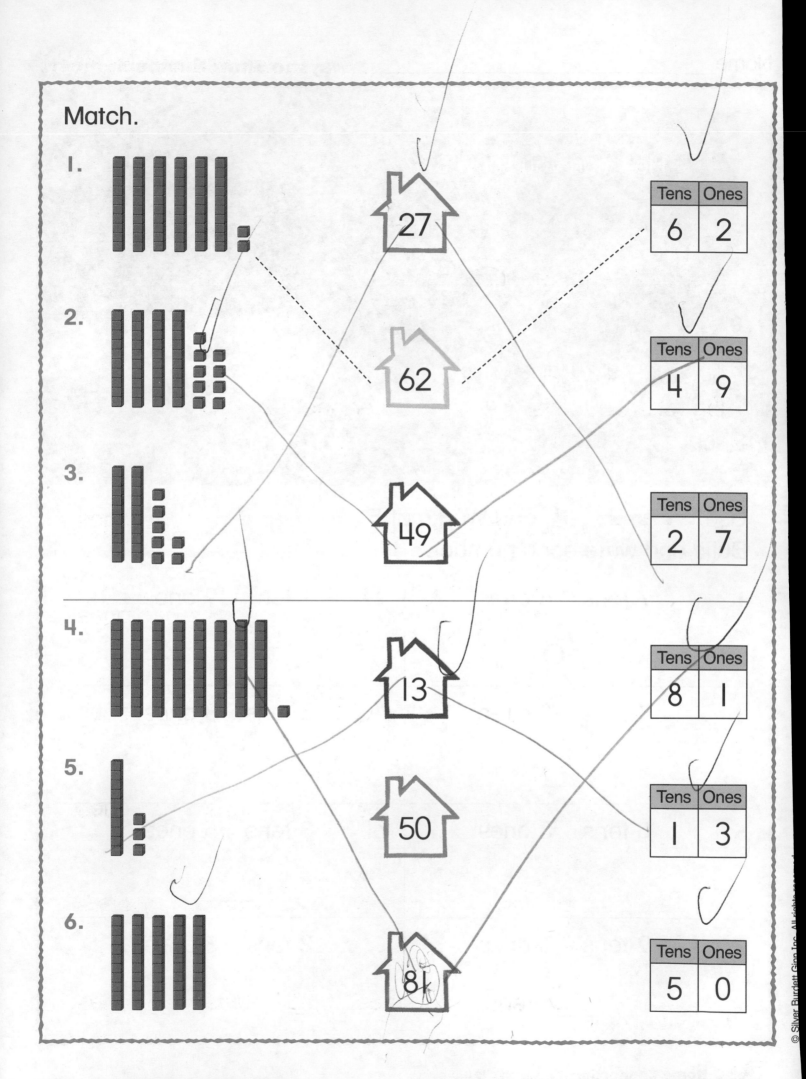

1.

2.

3.

4.

5.

6.

Tens	Ones
6	2

Tens	Ones
4	9

Tens	Ones
2	7

Tens	Ones
8	1

Tens	Ones
1	3

Tens	Ones
5	0

27

62

49

13

50

81

© Silver Burdett Ginn Inc. All rights reserved.

 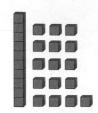 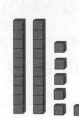

You can show 26 in different ways.

26 ones $= 1$ ten 16 ones $= 2$ tens 6 ones

Use ▭, ■, and Workmat 5.
Build each number one way.
Then regroup to show each number another way.
Record the ways.

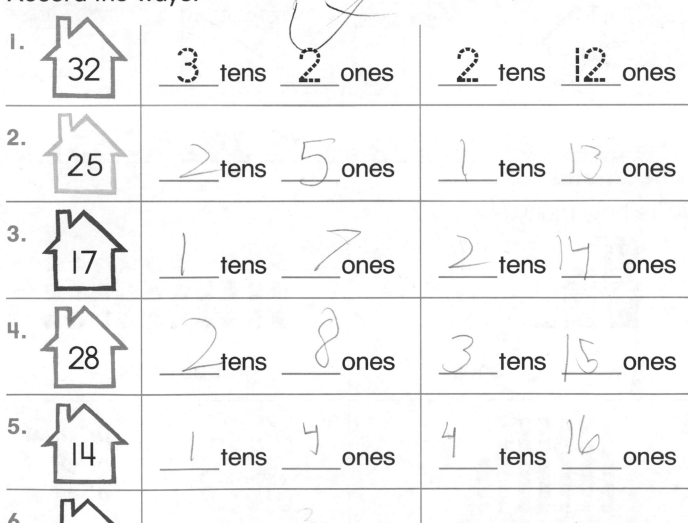

1. 32	3 tens	2 ones	2 tens	12 ones
2. 25	2 tens	5 ones	1 tens	13 ones
3. 17	1 tens	7 ones	2 tens	14 ones
4. 28	2 tens	8 ones	3 tens	15 ones
5. 14	1 tens	4 ones	4 tens	16 ones
6. 33	3 tens	3 ones	5 tens	17 ones

Home Connection Children use models to show the same number different ways. Ask your child to draw models to show numbers like 36 or 59 in two ways.

Use [ten-rod], [unit cube], and Workmat 5.
Build each number.
Regroup to show other ways.
Record the ways.

1. 32

Tens	Ones
3	2

Tens	Ones
2	3

Tens	Ones
3	2

2. 26

Tens	Ones
2	6

Tens	Ones
6	2

Tens	Ones
2	6

3. 45

Tens	Ones
4	5

Tens	Ones
5	4

Tens	Ones
4	5

Checkpoint

Write how many.

1. 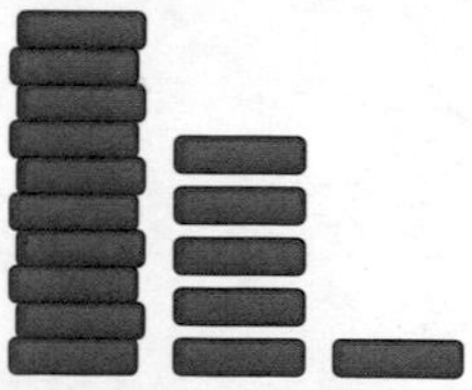

10 ten 1 ones 5

2. 

3 groups of ten = 26

3. 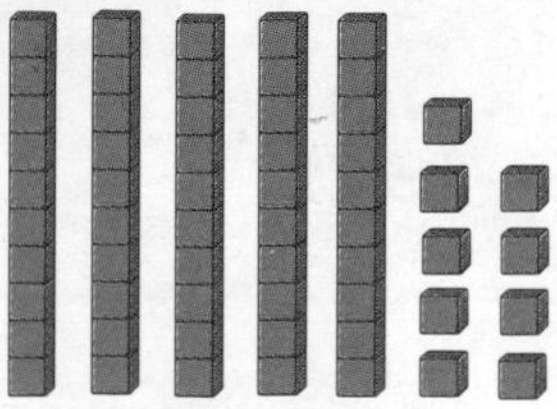

Tens	Ones
2	9

29

4. 
10
10
10
10
10
10

Tens	Ones
6	7

67

© Silver Burdett Ginn Inc. All rights reserved.

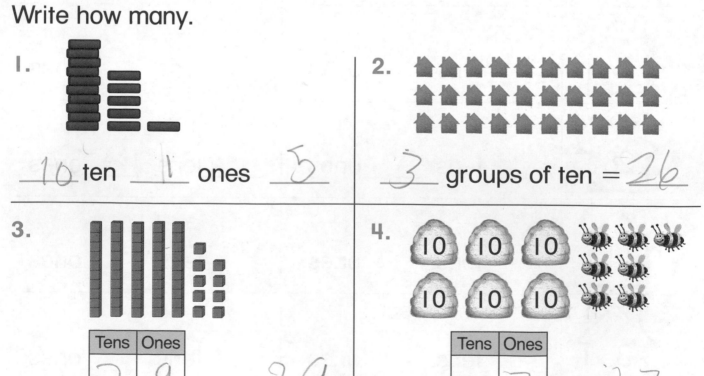

Name_____

Problem Solving
Guess and Check

STRATEGY
Understand
Plan
Look Back
Solve

The same number of birds lives in each of these houses. How many birds in each house?

12 in all

 Understand

You need to find how many birds live in each house.

Keep guessing until you find the correct answer.

 Plan

Guess. Then use counters to check.

 Solve

• Guess 2 birds in each house.

6 birds in all.
This is not enough birds.
This answer is not correct.

• Try 4 birds in each house.

12 birds in all.
This answer is correct.

 Look Back

How can you tell if your answer is correct?

 Home Connection Help your child solve problems by guessing the answer, checking, then using the guess to find the correct answer.

one hundred seventy-nine **179**

Use counters to guess and check.

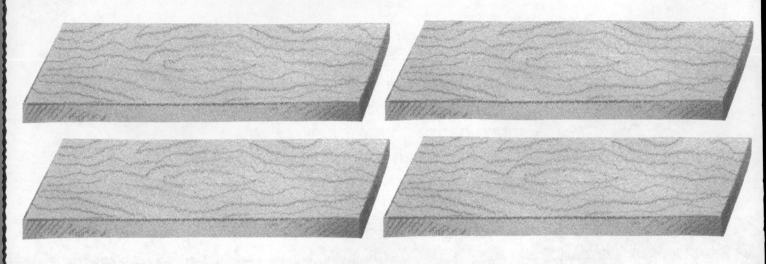

1. Matt has 12 books to put on 4 shelves. He wants to put the same number of books on each shelf. How many books go on each shelf?   _____ books

2. What if Matt has 15 books to put on 3 shelves? How many books would go on each shelf?   _____ books

3. What if Matt has only 10 books to put on 2 shelves? How many books would go on each shelf?   _____ books

 Critical Thinking Corner

Logical Thinking

Use guess and check to solve.

4. The shelter has 10 cats and dogs in all. There are 2 more cats than dogs. How many cats and dogs are there?

   _____ cats   _____ dogs

47 is before 48.

49 is after 48.

48 is between 47 and 49.

Write each number that comes after.

1.

32   33   34

2.

56   57   58

3.

75   76   77

4.

93   94   ___

Write each number that comes before.

5.

21   22   23

6.

66   67   68

7.

80   81   82

8.

98   99   100

Home Connection Invite your child to count with you from 1 to 100. Talk about numbers that come before, after, and between other numbers.

one hundred eighty-three   **183**

Write each number that comes between.

1.
45 46 47

2.
60 61 62

3.
13 14 15

4.
88 89 90

Write each number that comes before and after.

5.
37 38 39

6.
71 72 73

7.
98 99 100

8.
49 50 51

 Critical Thinking Corner

Using Algebra

Use the number line to solve.

80 81 82 83 84 85 86 87 88 89 90 91 92 93 94 95

9. Which number comes between 89 and 91? 90

10. Which number is greater than 85? 89

© Silver Burdett Ginn Inc. All rights reserved.

Name_____

1. Write the missing numbers.

2. Color numbers with 9 ones ⟨ green ⟩.

3. Color numbers with 0 ones ⟨ blue ⟩.

4. Color numbers with 2 tens ⟨ red ⟩.

You can find patterns in numbers.

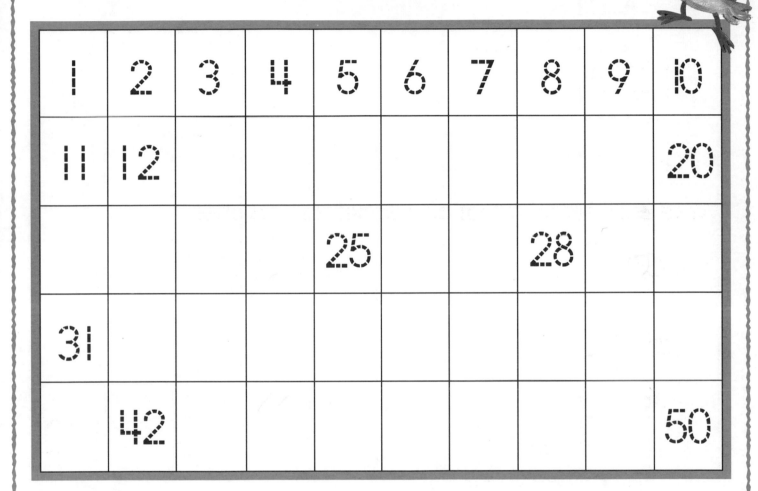

1	2	3	4	5	6	7	8	9	10
11	12								20
				25			28		
31									
	42								50

Use the chart to complete each pattern.

5. 1   3   5   7

6. 5   10   15   20   25   30   35

Home Connection Look at the chart with your child. Have your child tell you how numbers in one row change. Then talk about how numbers in one column change.

one hundred eighty-five   **185**

1. Write the missing numbers.

2. Color numbers with 3 ones red .

3. Color numbers with 6 tens blue .

4. Color numbers with 0 ones green .

51	52								
61									
				76					
81									
									100

Critical Thinking Corner

Visual Thinking

5. Look for other patterns on the chart.
   Use yellow to color one pattern.
   Tell about your pattern.

© Silver Burdett Ginn Inc. All rights reserved.

Word Bank
skip count

1. Skip count by twos.

2   4   ___   ___   ___

2. Skip count by fives.

5   10   ___   ___   ___

3. Skip count by tens.

10   20   ___   ___   ___

Home Connection Invite your child to skip count aloud by twos, fives, and tens. Help your child count to 50 or above.

one hundred eighty-seven   **187**

1. Skip count by twos. Circle the numbers.

2. Skip count by fives. Put an X on the numbers.

3. Skip count by tens. Color the numbers red.

1	2	3	4	5	6	7	8	9	10
11	12	13	14	15	16	17	18	19	20
21	22	23	24	25	26	27	28	29	30
31	32	33	34	35	36	37	38	39	40
41	42	43	44	45	46	47	48	49	50
51	52	53	54	55	56	57	58	59	60
61	62	63	64	65	66	67	68	69	70
71	72	73	74	75	76	77	78	79	80
81	82	83	84	85	86	87	88	89	90
91	92	93	94	95	96	97	98	99	100

4. Tell about the numbers that have only an X.

5. Tell about the numbers you colored red.

6. Tell about other patterns you see.

© Silver Burdett Ginn Inc. All rights reserved.

Problem Solving
Choosing Reasonable Answers

This is Tiwa.
She lives here.

Circle the number that makes sense.
Think: Use the picture to help you.

1. Tiwa's home has ⬭6⬭ or 60 rooms.

_____

2. There are 4 or 45 chairs in the kitchen.

_____

3. Tiwa's bedroom has 82 or 2 windows.

_____

4. There are 3 or 33 lamps in the living room.

_____

5. Grandfather is 7 or 75 years old.

_____

6. Mom reads a newspaper with 2 or 72 pages.

 Home Connection Your child is learning to choose reasonable answers. Ask your child similar word problems about your own home.

This is Jordan. He lives in this apartment building.

Circle the number that makes sense.

1. This building has 3 or (30) rooms.

_____

2. Jordan has 2 or 21   bathrooms in his apartment.

_____

3. There are 49 or 4   beds in his home.

_____

4. Jordan has 6 or 68   chairs in his living room.

_____

5. Jordan shares his home with 3 or 93   people.

_____

6. Jordan's little sister is 55 or 5   years old.

© Silver Burdett Ginn Inc. All rights reserved.

Name_____ **Checkpoint**

Circle the greater number.

1.   86   84 | 2.   63   69

Circle the number that is less.

3.   74   64 | 4.   32   23

Write the missing numbers.

5.
42   43   ___

6.
___   53   54

7.
36   ___   38

8.
___   87   ___

Skip count by twos.

9.

  2   4   ___   ___   ___   ___

Use guess and check to solve.

10. 6 birds live in 2 bird houses.
    2 more birds live in one house
    than in the other.
    How many birds live in each house?

    _____ birds   _____ birds

Connect the dots in order.
Start at 31.

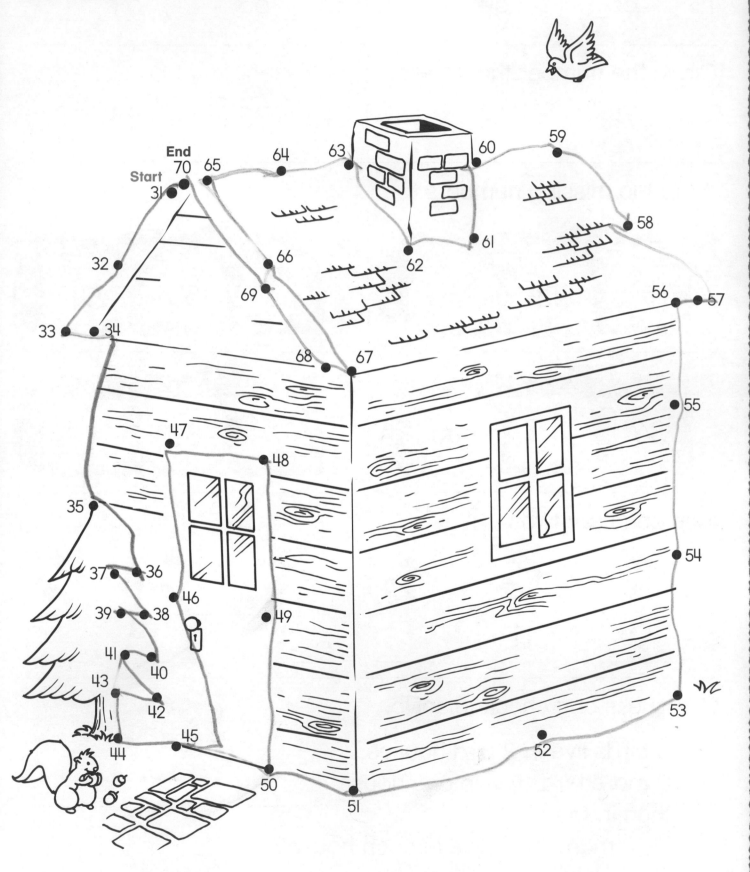

© Silver Burdett Ginn Inc. All rights reserved.

Name_____

Write how many.

1.

Tens	Ones

= _____

2.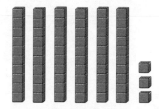

Tens	Ones

= _____

3. **46** _____ tens _____ ones

4. **89** _____ tens _____ ones

Write the missing numbers.

5.

25   26   _____

6.

_____   92   93

Circle **greater than** or **less than**.

7. 76 is   greater than   79.
            less than

8. 32 is   greater than   35.
            less than

Skip count by fives.

9.

5   10   _____   _____   _____   _____

Circle the number that makes sense.

10. Shannon drank   3   or   31   glasses of milk today.

Name_____ **Performance Assessment**

What You Need

tens   ones   Workmat 5

number cube

① Roll the number cube. Show that many tens.

② Roll again. Show that many ones.

③ Write how many tens and ones. Write how many in all.

1. ____ tens ____ ones ____ in all	2. ____ tens ____ ones ____ in all
3. ____ tens ____ ones ____ in all	4. ____ tens ____ ones ____ in all
5. ____ tens ____ ones ____ in all	6. ____ tens ____ ones ____ in all

Look at the numbers you recorded.

7. What is the greatest number? ____

8. What is the least number? ____

 For Your Portfolio
You might put this page in your portfolio.

© Silver Burdett Ginn Inc. All rights reserved.

Use the number cards below to make numbers.
Use two cards to make each number.
Write the greatest number.
Write the least number.

1.

85   45
greatest   least

2.

_____   _____
greatest   least

3.

_____   _____
greatest   least

4.

_____   _____
greatest   least

5.

_____   _____
greatest   least

You can use a  to show two-digit numbers.

Remember to enter the tens first!

5 tens and 6 ones

Press

Show each number on the .

Record the keys. Write the number.

1. 7 tens and 2 ones

   Press

    72

2. 1 one and 4 tens

   Press

   _____

3. 9 tens and 7 ones

   Press

   _____

4. 4 ones and 6 tens

   Press

   _____

5.

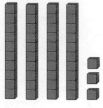

   Press

   _____

6.

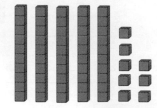

   Press

   _____

© Silver Burdett Ginn Inc. All rights reserved.

Fill in the ⬭ for the correct answer.
How many are there?

1.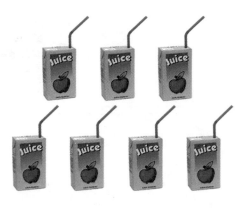

⬭ ⬭ ⬭ ⬭
7   6   8   5

2.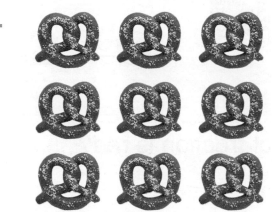

⬭ ⬭ ⬭ ⬭
8   9   10   7

Add or subtract.

3. 3
   + 5
   ⬭ 6
   ⬭ 8
   ⬭ 9
   ⬭ 7

4. 4
   + 2
   ⬭ 5
   ⬭ 4
   ⬭ 6
   ⬭ 7

5. 7
   − 5
   ⬭ 1
   ⬭ 3
   ⬭ 2
   ⬭ 4

6. 6
   − 3
   ⬭ 5
   ⬭ 3
   ⬭ 4
   ⬭ 2

7. 5
   + 5
   ⬭ 0
   ⬭ 10
   ⬭ 12
   ⬭ 1

8. 8
   − 1
   ⬭ 6
   ⬭ 7
   ⬭ 9
   ⬭ 10

9. 6
   + 6
   ⬭ 10
   ⬭ 12
   ⬭ 11
   ⬭ 13

10. 7
    − 2
    ⬭ 8
    ⬭ 6
    ⬭ 4
    ⬭ 5

11. 9
    + 2
    ⬭ 8
    ⬭ 10
    ⬭ 11
    ⬭ 12

Which has the same shape?

12.

⬯   ⬯

⬯   ⬯

13.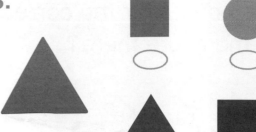

⬯   ⬯

⬯   ⬯

What fraction is red?

14.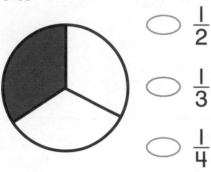

⬯ $\frac{1}{2}$

⬯ $\frac{1}{3}$

⬯ $\frac{1}{4}$

15.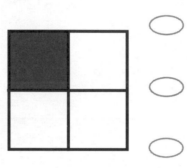

⬯ $\frac{1}{2}$

⬯ $\frac{1}{3}$

⬯ $\frac{1}{4}$

16.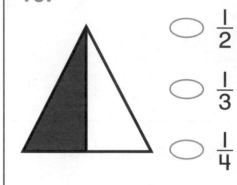

⬯ $\frac{1}{2}$

⬯ $\frac{1}{3}$

⬯ $\frac{1}{4}$

---

17. How many are there?

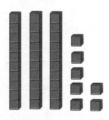

⬯ 27

⬯ 36

⬯ 37

⬯ 73

18. What number comes next?

72, 73, _____

◯   ◯   ◯   ◯

71   70   75   74

Solve.

19. I have curves.
I have faces.
What shape am I?

⬯   ⬯   ⬯

Which answer makes sense?

20. Franklin's family has
_____ cars.

⬯   ⬯   ⬯

2   25   52

© Silver Burdett Ginn Inc. All rights reserved.

Money

Silly Sam

written by

Eric Michaels

illustrated by

Stephen Carpenter

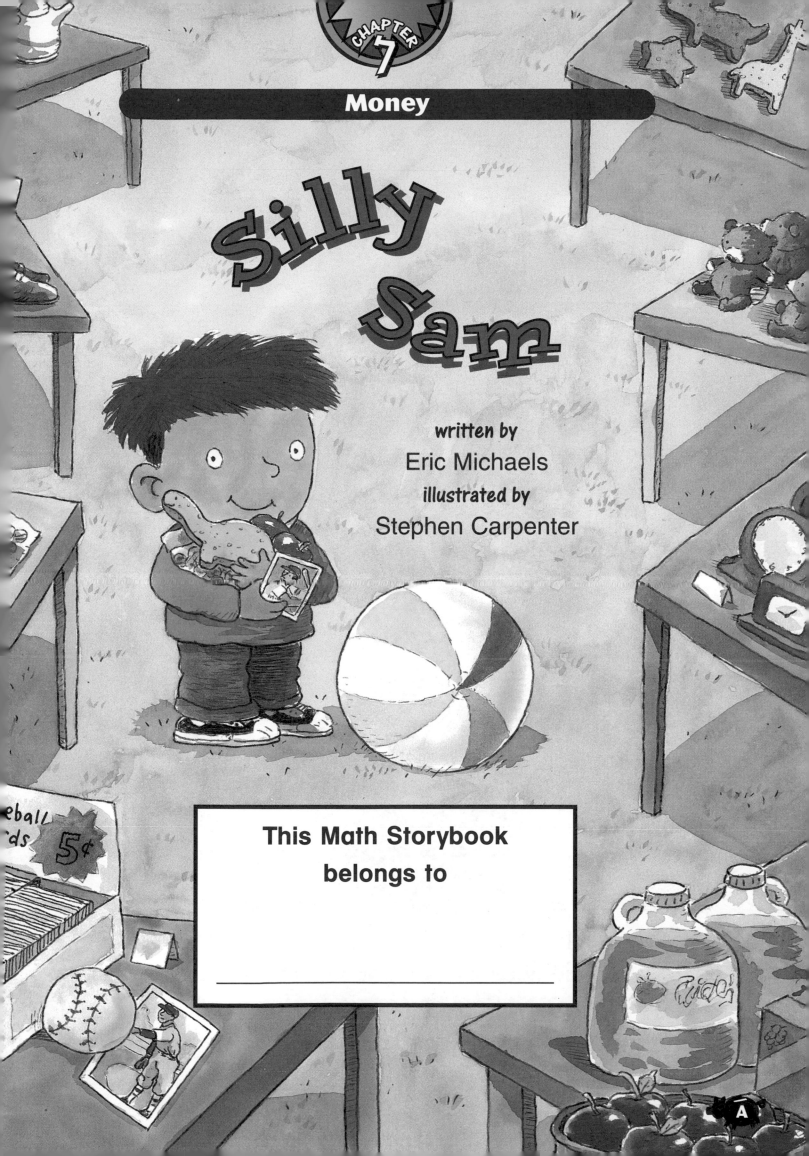

This Math Storybook

belongs to

_____

A

Sam loves Saturdays.
He goes shopping with his brother.
Today, Sam has a quarter to spend.

© Silver Burdett Ginn Inc. All rights reserved.

Sam wants marbles.
He puts his quarter on the table.
"What a deal!" he says.

"Silly Sam!" says his brother.
"You forgot your change!
You paid 25¢, but the marbles only cost 15¢.
You get a dime back."

Sam wants a baseball card.
He puts his dime on the table.
"What a deal!" he says.

"Silly Sam!" says his brother.
"You forgot your change!
You paid 10¢, but the card only costs 5¢.
You get a nickel back."

© Silver Burdett Ginn Inc. All rights reserved.

D

Sam wants a silly sponge.
He puts his nickel on the table.
"What a deal!" he says.

"Silly Sam!" says his brother.
"You forgot your change!
You paid 5¢, but the sponge only costs 2¢.
You get 3 pennies back."

Sam wants a snack.
He puts his three pennies on the table.
The woman gives him two apples.

"Smart Sam!" says his brother.
"What a deal!" says Sam.

What You Need

2 pennies

2 nickels

2 dimes

2 quarters

1. Use the boxes to sort the coins.
   Make as many groups as you like.

2. Then sort another way.
   Tell about ways to group the coins.
   Can you sort another way?

Home Connection Children learn that coins can be sorted by attributes such as size and color. Give your child a handful of coins and ask him or her to sort them in different ways.

one hundred ninety-nine   **199**

Put an X on the coins that are not the same kind.

1.

2.

3.

4.

© Silver Burdett Ginn Inc. All rights reserved.

or  or

penny
1¢

I nickel equals
5 pennies.

nickel
5¢

Word Bank
penny
nickel

Count on. Write how much in all.

1.

1¢   2¢   3¢   4¢   5¢   5¢
_____   _____
                                    in all

2.

5¢   10¢   15¢   20¢   25¢   25¢
_____   _____
                                    in all

3.

5¢   10¢   11¢   12¢   13¢   13¢
_____   _____
                                    in all

4.

5¢   10¢   16¢   12¢   13¢   14¢
_____   _____
                                    in all

Home Connection Give your child a set of coins containing nickels
and pennies. Have him or her determine the total value of each set.

Circle the coins to match each price.

1.

6¢

2.

9¢

3.

12¢

4.

15¢

© Silver Burdett Ginn Inc. All rights reserved.

![Problem Solving](PROBLEM SOLVING) **Problem Solving**

Solve.

5. Carol has 3 nickels and 3 pennies.
   How much money does she have?

   18 ¢

   Can she buy the toy frog?
   Explain.

20¢

202 two hundred two

Name_____ **Pennies and Dimes**

  or

 or

penny

dime

I¢

I dime equals
10 pennies.

10¢

Word Bank

dime

Count on. Write how much in all.

1.

10¢ 20¢ 30¢ 40¢ 50¢   50¢
____ ____ ____ ____ ____   ____
                               in all

2.

10¢ 20¢ 30¢ 40¢ 50¢ 60¢   60¢
____ ____ ____ ____ ____ ____   ____
                                    in all

3.

10¢ 20¢ 30¢ 31¢ 32¢ 33¢   33¢
____ ____ ____ ____ ____ ____   ____
                                    in all

4.

10¢ 20¢ 21¢ 22¢ 23¢ 24¢   24¢
____ ____ ____ ____ ____ ____   ____
                                    in all

 Home Connection Children learn to count coins by counting on from each coin. Give your child sets of coins containing pennies and dimes. Have your child count the coins.

two hundred three **203**

Circle the coins to match each price.

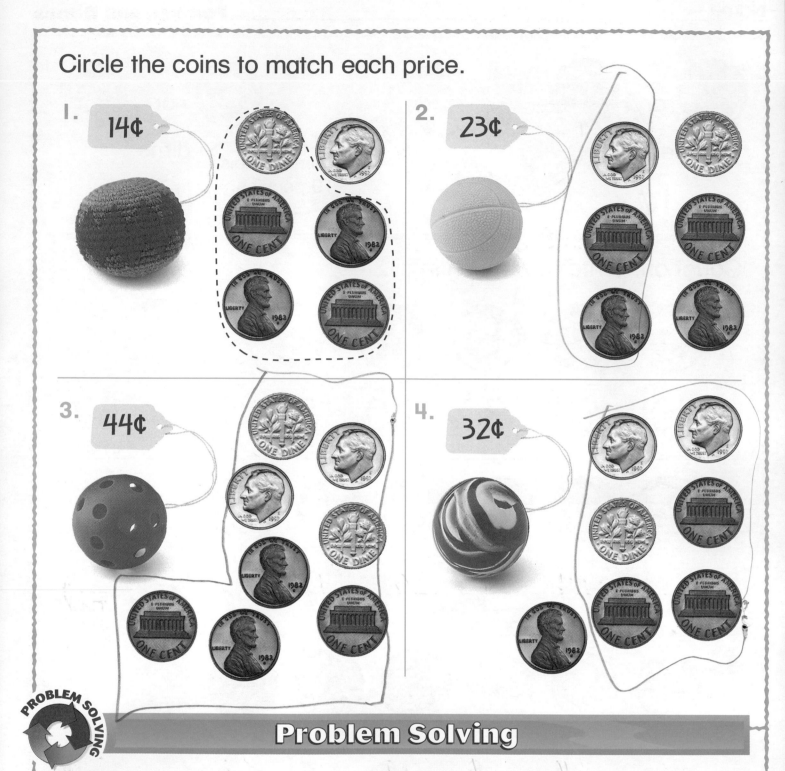

1. 14¢

2. 23¢

3. 44¢

4. 32¢

Solve.

5. You have pennies and dimes.
   You pick up 3 coins.
   What is the greatest amount you could have? ___B___¢

   What is the least amount you could have? __50__¢

© Silver Burdett Ginn Inc. All rights reserved.

To count coins, start with the coins of greatest value.

22¢

Count on.
Write how much you have in all.

1.

5¢   10¢   15¢   20¢   21¢   22¢   22¢
in all

2.

10¢   20¢   30¢   40¢   41¢   41¢
in all

3.

10¢   5¢   10¢   20¢   26¢   22¢   22¢
in all

4.

10¢   5¢   10¢   11¢   12¢   13¢   13¢
in all

 Home Connection Children learn that when counting a set of coins it is easier to start with the coin of greatest value. Have your child count sets of coins containing pennies, nickels, and dimes.

Remember to start with the coin of greatest value.

Write each amount.

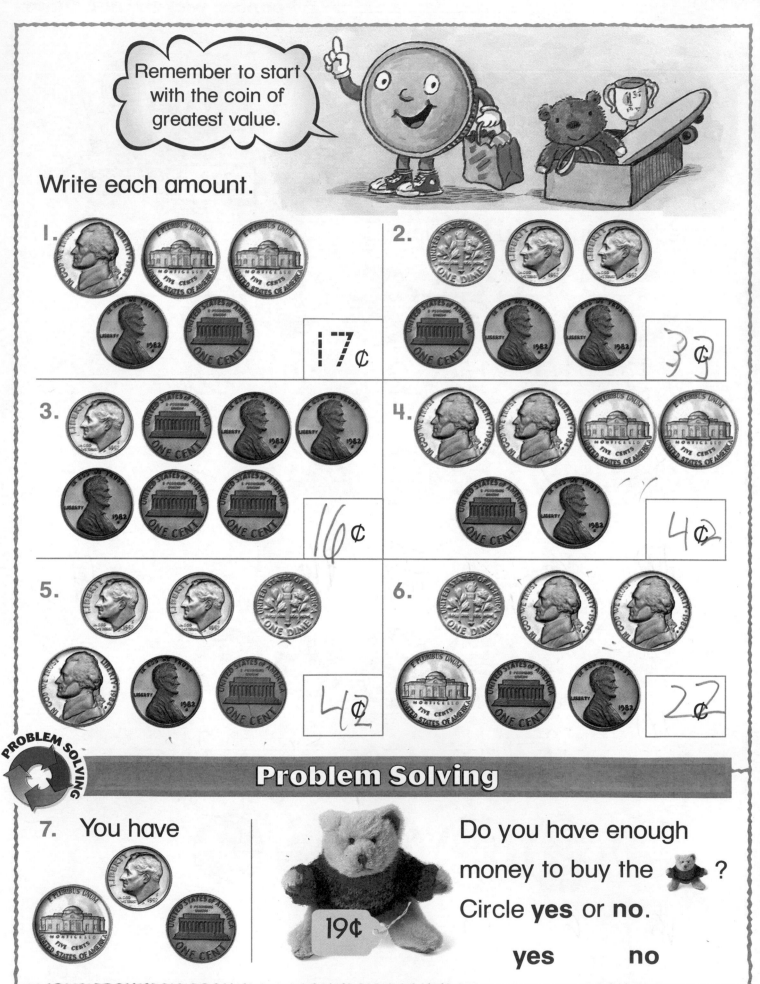

1. 17¢

2. 39¢

3. 16¢

4. 4¢

5. 4¢

6. 22¢

Problem Solving

7. You have

Do you have enough money to buy the ?
Circle **yes** or **no**.

19¢

yes   no

© Silver Burdett Ginn Inc. All rights reserved.

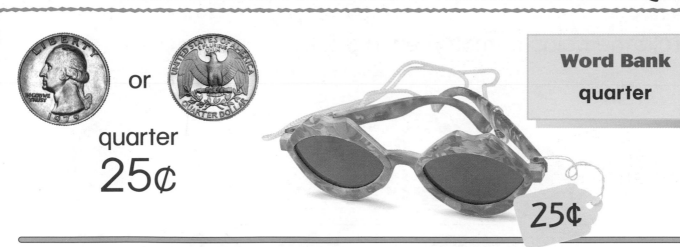

or

quarter

25¢

Word Bank

quarter

25¢

Circle the coins you could trade for a quarter.

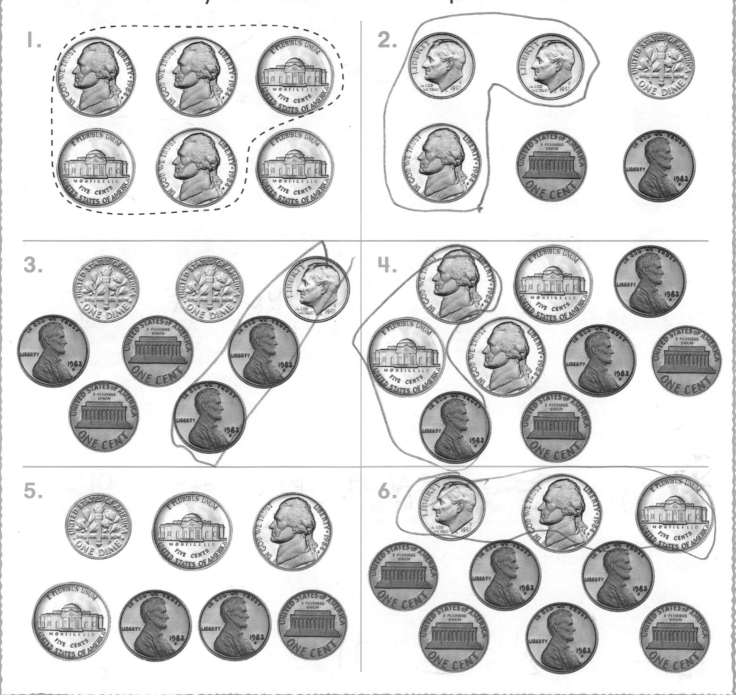

1.

2.

3.

4.

5.

6.

Home Connection Have your child take and count
a handful of coins. Encourage your child to explain the
order in which he or she counted the coins and why.

two hundred seven   **207**

Circle the coins to match each price.

1. 25¢

2. 35¢

3. 26¢

4. 25¢

 Critical Thinking Corner

Logical Thinking

5. You have 3 coins.
   They equal a quarter.
   Draw the coins you have.

© Silver Burdett Ginn Inc. All rights reserved

Name_____

Count the coins.
Write how much in all.

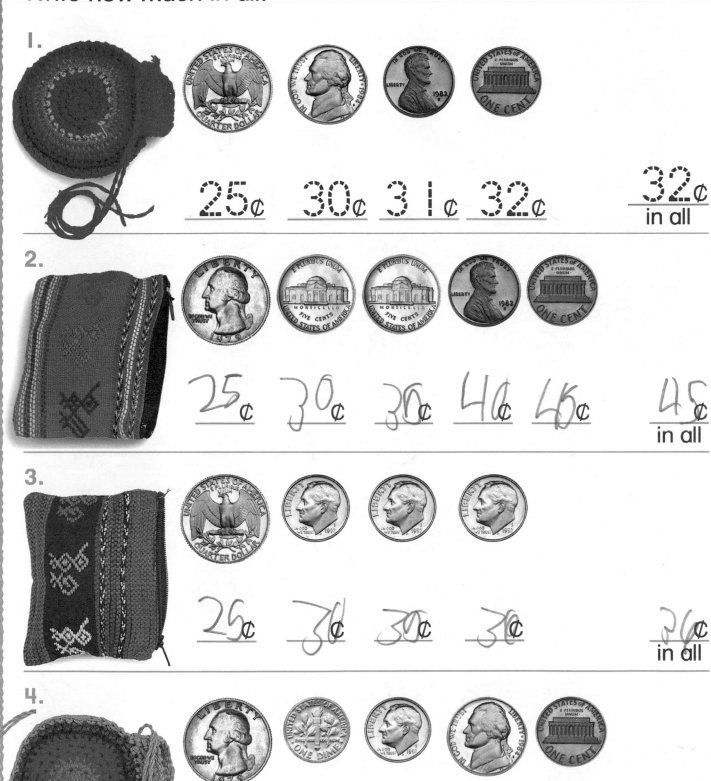

1. 25¢   30¢   31¢   32¢   32¢
                                in all

2. 25¢   30¢   35¢   40¢   45¢   45¢
                                in all

3. 25¢   35¢   30¢   30¢   35¢
                                in all

4. 25¢   30¢   36¢   37¢   38¢   38¢
                                in all

Home Connection Have your child empty a coin purse. Ask him or her to count five of the coins and tell you how much money there is.

Circle the coins to show how much.

1. 22¢

2. 45¢

3. 15¢

 Checkpoint

1. Count on.
   Write how much in all.

25¢   30¢   35¢   40¢   45¢   50¢   50¢
                                                    in all

2. Circle the coins to match the price.

41¢

© Silver Burdett Ginn Inc. All rights reserved.

Name _____ **Choosing Coins**

THERE'S ALWAYS A WAY!

What coins could you use to buy one item?

I would use 2 dimes and 3 pennies!

I would use 4 nickels and 3 pennies!

23¢ each

Use coins.
Trace or draw coins to match each price.

1.

32¢

2.

48¢

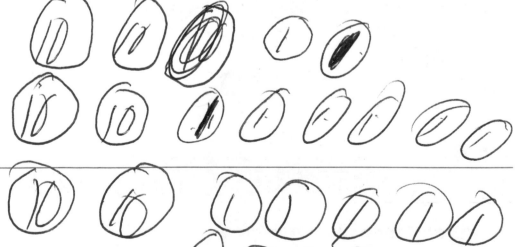

3.
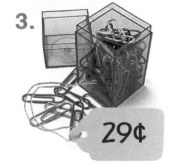
29¢

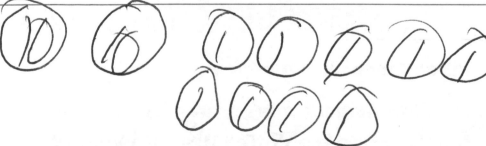

Home Connection Children need to practice combining different coins to get the same amount. Give your child a handful of coins and encourage him or her to use different coins to make a given amount.

two hundred eleven **211**

Use coins to solve.
How much more money
do you need to buy each item?
Draw or trace the coins you need.

1.

43¢

2.

36¢

3.

50¢

Critical Thinking Corner

Using Algebra

Number Sense **Journal Idea**

 Can every amount be shown in more
than one way? Tell why or why not.

© Silver Burdett Ginn Inc. All rights reserved.

Name_____

Problem Solving
Make a Table

STRATEGY
Understand
Plan
Solve
Look Back

I have pennies and nickels.
I pick 3 coins.
How much money could I have?

Understand

You need to find all possible groups
of 3 coins.

Plan

You can make a table.
Use pennies and nickels to
make groups of 3 coins.

Solve

		Total Amount
3	0	3¢
2	1	¢
1	2	¢
0	3	¢

The boy could have __3¢, ___¢, ___¢, or ___¢.

Look Back

Find patterns in the table.
How do the patterns help you solve the problem?

Home Connection Look for tables in newspapers or magazines. Discuss with your child how tables oraganize information.

two hundred thirteen   213

Use and .

Complete each table.

I have 2 coins. How much money could I have?

1.

		Total Amount
2	0	2 ¢
1		¢
0		¢

I have 4 coins. How much money could I have?

2.

		Amount
4	0	4 ¢
	1	¢
2		¢
	3	¢
0		¢

© Silver Burdett Ginn Inc. All rights reserved.

35¢ is more than 24¢.

35¢   24¢

Count the coins.
Write each amount.
Circle the group that is worth more.

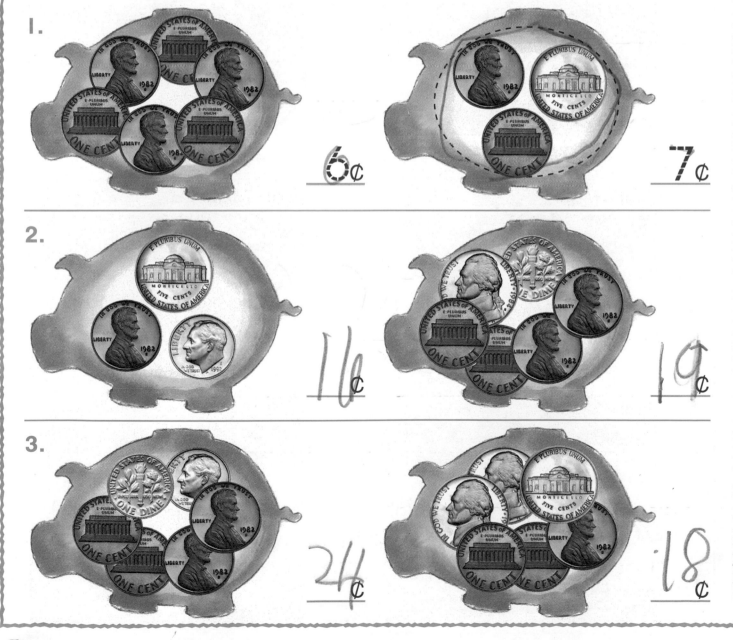

1.   6¢   7¢

2.   16¢   19¢

3.   24¢   18¢

 Home Connection As children compare groups of coins, they begin to understand that more coins do not necessarily mean greater value. Give your child groups of coins to compare values.

two hundred fifteen **215**

Count the coins.
Write each amount.
Circle the group that shows less.

1.

 _____ ¢

 _____ ¢

2.

 _____ ¢

 _____ ¢

3.

 _____ ¢

 _____ ¢

What Do You Think?

Journal Idea

 I think having a dime is better than having a penny, even though a dime is smaller. What do you think?

© Silver Burdett Ginn Inc. All rights reserved.

Name_____

APPLICATION
Understand
Plan
Look Back
Solve

Problem Solving
Making Purchases

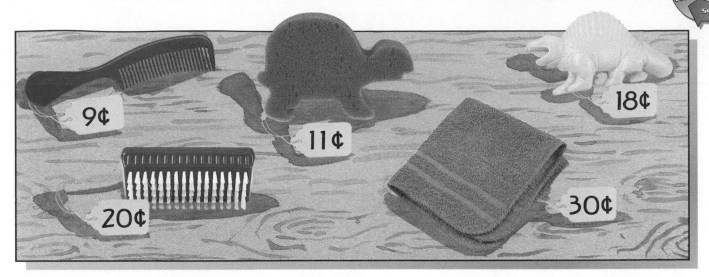

9¢ 11¢ 18¢ 20¢ 30¢

Write how much money you have.
Circle what you would buy.
Think: Use the picture to find the prices.

1.     10¢

2.    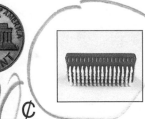   20¢

3.     ___¢

4.      ___¢

 Home Connection Give your child a handful of coins. Set up a home store and have your child purchase different items.

40¢   25¢   27¢

6¢   19¢   31¢

Write how much money you have.
Circle what you would buy.

1.  6¢

2. _____ ¢

3. _____ ¢

4.  _____ ¢

© Silver Burdett Ginn Inc. All rights reserved.

1. Trace or draw coins to match the price.

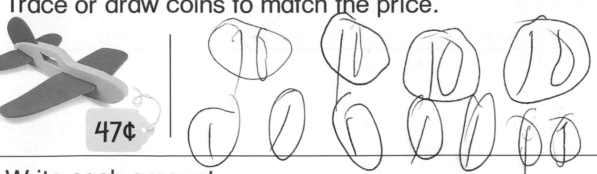

47¢

2. Write each amount.
   Circle the group that is worth less.

15¢

9¢

3. Write each amount.
   Circle the group that is worth more.

8¢

5¢

4. Add or subtract.

7¢	8¢	9¢	4¢	9¢	7¢
+5¢	−6¢	−4¢	+0¢	+2¢	−4¢
¢	¢	5¢	4¢	11¢	3¢

5. Write the amount. Circle what you can buy.

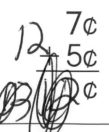   

40¢   30¢

30¢

Name_____

You want to buy each item.
How many of each coin would you use?
Use coins. Write how many.

Item	 (quarter)	 (dime)	 (nickel)	 (penny)
1. 46¢ 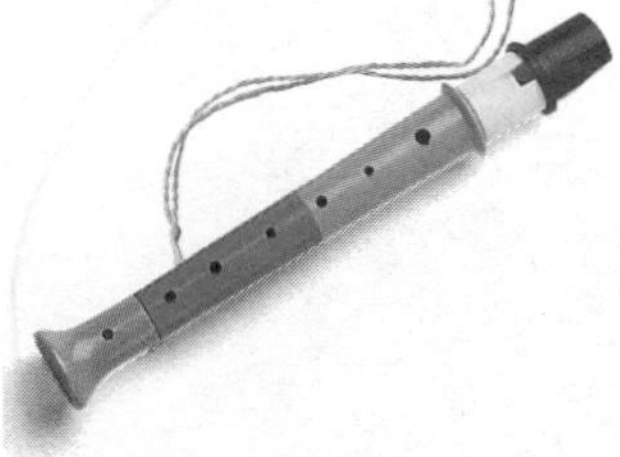	1	2	0	1
2. 32¢ 	1			
3. 40¢ 				
4. 33¢ 				

© Silver Burdett Ginn Inc. All rights reserved.

Relating Addition and Subtraction

Behind the Door

written by Roscoe Murphy

illustrated by Terry Kovalcik

This Math Storybook

belongs to

Alton

Behind the big white door,
it's time to start the day.
12 eggs are in a carton.
6 climb out to play.

© Silver Burdett Ginn Inc. All rights reserved.

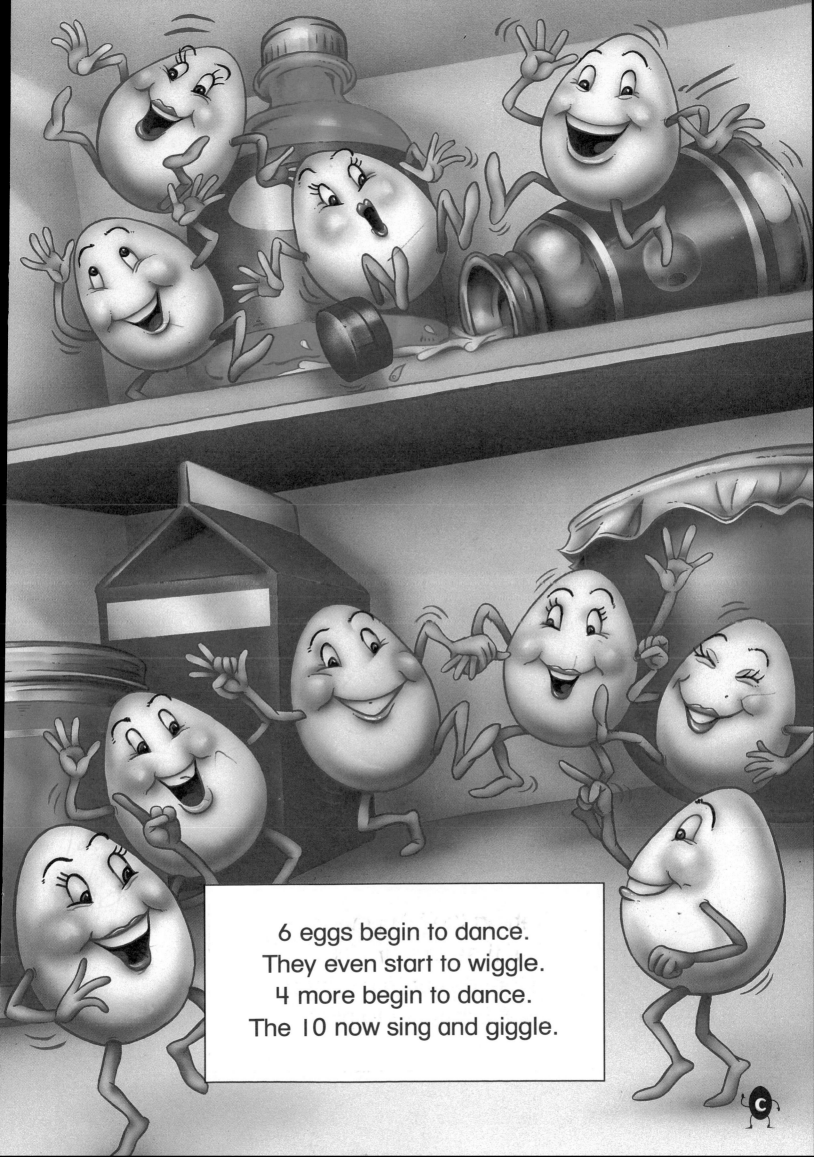

6 eggs begin to dance.
They even start to wiggle.
4 more begin to dance.
The 10 now sing and giggle.

8 eggs take turns jumping,
some are upside down.
Look at all the many ways
the 8 bounce up and down.

© Silver Burdett Ginn Inc. All rights reserved.

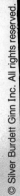

7 eggs use a carrot
to play on and to climb.
2 begin to slide right down.
How many wait in line?

© Silver Burdett Ginn Inc. All rights reserved.

Draw some eggs on the shelf
and some more just below.
Then tell a number story
of how eggs come and go.

20 + 20 = 40

A Note to the Family

Here are some learning ideas you can share with your child.

Enjoy *Behind the Door* Together

- Read the story aloud with your child. Talk about all the things the eggs do to have fun. Encourage your child to count the different groups of eggs on each page, then tell addition and subtraction stories about each picture.

- Encourage your child to show you what she or he drew on the last page of *Behind the Door*. Then work together to add and subtract the two groups of eggs. Have your child write the addition and subtraction sentences. For example, if your child drew a group of 6 eggs and a group of 4 eggs, he or she could write

$$6 + 4 = 10 \text{ and } 10 - 6 = 4.$$

At-Home Activity

- Have your child put 12 apples, oranges, pieces of play food, or other small items in different groups to practice adding and subtracting to and from 12. Write the addition or subtraction sentences as your child groups the objects. Then ask your child to complete each sentence.

Read More About It!

To read more about subtraction with your child, look for these books in your local library.

- *The Baker's Dozen: A Colonial American Tale* by Heather Forest (HarcourtBrace Juvenile Books, 1993)

- *Mr. Grumpy's Outing* by John Burningham (Holt, 1990)

- *12 Ways to Get to 11* by Eve Merriam (Simon & Schuster, 1993)

Visit Our Web Site!

INTERNET ACTIVITY
www.sbgmath.com

© Silver Burdett Ginn Inc. All rights reserved.

5 + 2 = 7

7 – 2 = 5

Use two colors of cubes and
Workmat 4. Show each number.
Write an addition sentence.
Write a subtraction sentence.

1. 6 and 2 | 6 + 2 = 8 | 8 – 2 = 6

2. 4 and 3 | ___ + ___ = ___ | ___ – ___ = ___

3. 5 and 6 | ___ + ___ = ___ | ___ – ___ = ___

4. 8 and 4 | ___ + ___ = ___ | ___ – ___ = ___

5. 5 and 7 | ___ + ___ = ___ | ___ – ___ = ___

Home Connection It is important for children to understand
that addition and subtraction are related. Ask your child to make
up related addition and subtraction stories about 12 pennies.

two hundred twenty-seven   **227**

Add and subtract.

1.

$3 + 7 = \underline{10}$

$10 - 7 = \underline{3}$

2.

$4 + 5 = \underline{9}$

$9 - 5 = \underline{4}$

3.

$6 + 3 = \underline{9}$

$9 - 3 = \underline{6}$

4.

$5 + 6 = \underline{11}$

$11 - 6 = \underline{5}$

What Do You Think?

Journal Idea

I think the picture shows $5 + 5$. You think it shows $10 - 5$. Who is right? Explain.

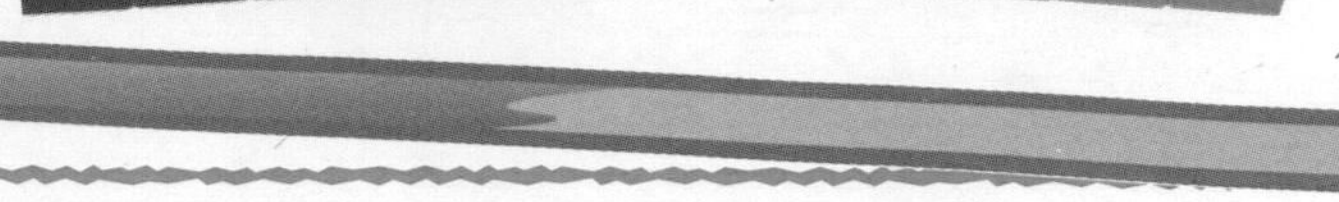

© Silver Burdett Ginn Inc. All rights reserved.

What addition fact can
help you find $11 - 7$?

$$11$$
$$-\ 7$$
$$\overline{\ \ 4}$$

$7 + 4 = 11,$
so $11 - 7 = 4.$

Word Bank
related fact

Circle the related addition fact.
Then subtract.

1.
$$\begin{array}{r} 12 \\ -\ 7 \\ \hline 5 \end{array}$$

$7 + 3 = 10$

$7 + 4 = 11$

$(7 + 5 = 12)$

2.
$$\begin{array}{r} 10 \\ -\ 6 \\ \hline 5 \end{array}$$

$(6 + 4 = 10)$

$6 + 5 = 11$

$6 + 6 = 12$

3.
$$\begin{array}{r} 11 \\ -\ 5 \\ \hline 4 \end{array}$$

$5 + 5 = 10$

$(5 + 6 = 11)$

$5 + 7 = 12$

4.
$$\begin{array}{r} 9 \\ -\ 4 \\ \hline 3 \end{array}$$

$(4 + 5 = 9)$

$5 + 3 = 8$

$5 + 5 = 10$

5.
$$\begin{array}{r} 12 \\ -\ 8 \\ \hline 4 \end{array}$$

$8 + 2 = 10$

$8 + 3 = 11$

$(8 + 4 = 12)$

6.
$$\begin{array}{r} 10 \\ -\ 3 \\ \hline 7 \end{array}$$

$3 + 9 = 12$

$(3 + 7 = 10)$

$3 + 8 = 11$

Home Connection Your child is learning to use addition to
solve related subtraction problems. Give your child a subtraction
problem. Then challenge your child to think of a related addition fact.

Write a related addition fact.
Then subtract.

1. $12 - 8 = $ __4__   ____ $+$ __4__ $=$ __12__

2. $7 - 3 = $ __4__   __3__ $+$ __4__ $=$ __7__

3. $10 - 8 = $ __8__   __10__ $+$ __8__ $=$ __18__

4. $8 - 6 = $ __6__   __6__ $+$ __1__ $=$ __4__

5. $9 - 1 = $ __8__   __9__ $+$ __1__ $=$ __10__

6. $11 - 3 = $ __8__   __8__ $+$ __3__ $=$ __11__

Problem Solving

Solve.

7. Carolyn has 10 🥕 to feed the horses.

   One horse eats 2 🥕.

   Another horse eats 3 🥕.

   Erin gives Carolyn 5 more 🥕.

   How many 🥕 does Carolyn have now? ____ 🥕

© Silver Burdett Ginn Inc. All rights reserved

This is a fact family.

$3 + 7 = \underline{10}$ $\quad$ $10 - 7 = \underline{3}$

$7 + 3 = \underline{10}$ $\quad$ $10 - 3 = \underline{7}$

Complete each fact family.
Use counters if you like.

1.
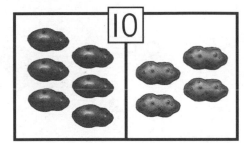

10

$6 + 4 = \underline{}$ $\quad$ $10 - 4 = \underline{}$

$4 + 6 = \underline{}$ $\quad$ $10 - 6 = \underline{}$

2.
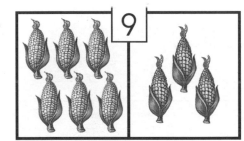

9

$6 + 3 = \underline{}$ $\quad$ $9 - 3 = \underline{}$

$3 + 6 = \underline{}$ $\quad$ $9 - 6 = \underline{}$

3.

7

$4 + 3 = \underline{}$ $\quad$ $7 - 3 = \underline{}$

$3 + 4 = \underline{}$ $\quad$ $7 - 4 = \underline{}$

4.

10

$5 + 5 = \underline{}$ $\quad$ $10 - 5 = \underline{}$

Home Connection Ask your child to write the fact family with the numbers 4, 5, and 9. Your child may use buttons or other household items to help.

two hundred thirty-one **231**

Add or subtract.
Use counters if you like.

1.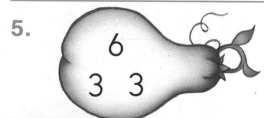
    10
    2 8

    $2 + 8 = 12$ $10 - 8 = \underline{}$

    $8 + 2 = \underline{}$ $10 - 2 = \underline{}$

2. 8
    4 4

    $4 + 4 = \underline{}$ $8 - 4 = \underline{}$

3. 9
    5 4

    $5 + 4 = \underline{}$ $9 - 4 = \underline{}$

    $4 + 5 = \underline{}$ $9 - 5 = \underline{}$

4. 10
    1 9

    $9 + 1 = \underline{}$ $10 - 1 = \underline{}$

    $1 + 9 = \underline{}$ $10 - 9 = \underline{}$

5. 6
    3 3

    $3 + 3 = \underline{}$ $6 - 3 = \underline{}$

Critical Thinking Corner

Number Sense **Journal Idea**

Look back at the exercises on this page.
Are there the same number of facts
in each fact family?
Tell why or why not.

© Silver Burdett Ginn Inc. All rights reserved.

What numbers are in this fact family?

7 + 4 = 11   11 − 4 = 7

4 + 7 = 11   11 − 7 = 4

Complete each fact family.

1.
___ + ___ = 11   11 − ___ = ___

___ + ___ = 11   11 − ___ = ___

2.
___ + ___ = 11   11 − ___ = ___

___ + ___ = 11   11 − ___ = ___

3.
___ + ___ = 11   11 − ___ = ___

___ + ___ = 11   11 − ___ = ___

4.
___ + ___ = 10   10 − ___ = ___

___ + ___ = 10   10 − ___ = ___

Home Connection Give your child 11 household items. Ask him or her to make 2 groups and write the fact family to describe the groups.

two hundred thirty-three   **233**

Complete each fact family.

1.
$$\begin{array}{r} 8 \\ + 2 \\ \hline 10 \end{array}$$
$$\begin{array}{r} 2 \\ + 8 \\ \hline 10 \end{array}$$
$$\begin{array}{r} 10 \\ - 8 \\ \hline 2 \end{array}$$
$$\begin{array}{r} 10 \\ - 2 \\ \hline 8 \end{array}$$

2.
$$\begin{array}{r} 5 \\ + 4 \\ \hline 9 \end{array}$$
$$\begin{array}{r} 4 \\ + 5 \\ \hline 9 \end{array}$$
$$\begin{array}{r} 9 \\ - 5 \\ \hline 4 \end{array}$$
$$\begin{array}{r} 9 \\ - 4 \\ \hline 5 \end{array}$$

3.
$$\begin{array}{r} 2 \\ + 9 \\ \hline 11 \end{array}$$
$$\begin{array}{r} 9 \\ + 2 \\ \hline 11 \end{array}$$
$$\begin{array}{r} 11 \\ - 2 \\ \hline 9 \end{array}$$
$$\begin{array}{r} 11 \\ - 9 \\ \hline 2 \end{array}$$

4.
$$\begin{array}{r} 4 \\ + 6 \\ \hline 10 \end{array}$$
$$\begin{array}{r} 6 \\ + 4 \\ \hline 10 \end{array}$$
$$\begin{array}{r} 10 \\ - 4 \\ \hline 6 \end{array}$$
$$\begin{array}{r} 10 \\ - 6 \\ \hline 4 \end{array}$$

Problem Solving

Solve.

5. Jack gave away all of his .

He gave 6 to Mandy.

Then he gave Kevin the other 5.

How many did he have to start? __11__

© Silver Burdett Ginn Inc. All rights reserved.

Name_____   **Fact Families to 12**

Add or subtract.

1.

7	5	12	12
+ 5	+ 7	− 7	− 5
12	12	5	7

2.

8	4	12	12
+ 4	+ 8	− 8	− 4
12	12	4	8

3.

9	3	12	12
+ 3	+ 9	− 9	− 3
12	12	3	9

4.

7	4	11	11
+ 4	+ 7	− 7	− 4
11	11	4	7

5.

6	12
+ 6	− 6
12	6

6 and 6 make one dozen.

Home Connection Give your child 12 pennies or other household items. Ask him or her to use the items to show several different fact families for 12.

Write the number sentences for each fact family.

1. $\underline{5} + \underline{6} = \underline{11}$ ___ − ___ = ___

    11
    6   5

    ___ + ___ = ___   ___ − ___ = ___

2. 10
    2   8

    ___ + ___ = ___   ___ − ___ = ___

    ___ + ___ = ___   ___ − ___ = ___

3. 12
    4   8

    ___ + ___ = ___   ___ − ___ = ___

    ___ + ___ = ___   ___ − ___ = ___

Checkpoint

Circle the related addition fact. Then subtract.

1. $\begin{array}{r} 12 \\ -\ 6 \\ \hline \end{array}$ $6 + 4 = 10$

   $7 + 5 = 12$

   $6 + 6 = 12$

2. $\begin{array}{r} 11 \\ -\ 9 \\ \hline \end{array}$ $9 + 1 = 10$

   $9 + 2 = 11$

   $7 + 4 = 11$

3. Complete the fact family.

   $3 + 7 = \underline{\hphantom{00}}$ $10 - 7 = \underline{\hphantom{00}}$

   $7 + 3 = \underline{\hphantom{00}}$ $10 - 3 = \underline{\hphantom{00}}$

© Silver Burdett Ginn Inc. All rights reserved.

$$10 - 2$$

$$6 + 2$$

$$5 + 3$$

I can name 8 in many ways. Can you think of another way?

Circle the names for each number.
Use counters if you like.

1.
3

(4 − 1)   3 + 2   8 + 3
2 + 2   (9 − 6)   (1 + 2)

2.
7

10 − 2   7 + 0   12 − 5
3 + 4   5 + 6   11 − 4

3.
6

3 + 3   12 − 6   9 − 4
7 − 1   6 + 3   4 + 2

4.
9

11 − 2   9 − 0   5 + 3
12 − 6   5 + 5   4 + 5

Home Connection Your child is learning different ways to name or make a number. Ask her or him to show different names for 10 and for 5. You may wish to use buttons or other household items to help.

Circle the names for each number.
Then write another name for each number.

1.
9

$(12 - 3)$ $(7 + 2)$ $9 - 3$

$4 + 4$ $(6 + 3)$ $(4 \oplus 5)$

2.
5

$8 + 4$ $8 - 3$ $9 + 3$

$6 - 1$ $4 + 1$ ___○___

3.
8

$8 + 0$ $6 + 5$ $11 - 3$

$4 + 3$ $12 - 4$ ___○___

4.
11

$11 - 4$ $12 - 9$ $7 + 4$

$9 + 2$ $3 + 8$ ___○___

What Do You Think?

Journal Idea

I can think of 6 names for 4.
How many can you think of?
Tell what they are.

© Silver Burdett Ginn Inc. All rights reserved.

APPLICATION
Understand
Plan
Look Back
Solve

Problem Solving
Choose the Operation

Name_____

Jon has 6 . He eats 3.

How many are left?

Think: Do you need to add

or subtract?

$$6 + 3 = \underline{}$$

$$6 - 3 = 3$$

Circle the correct number sentence.
Then solve.

1. Chen has 3 .

    He picks 2 more.

    How many does
    he have now?

    $$3 - 2 = \underline{}$$

    $$3 + 2 = \underline{}$$

2. Marco has 9 .

    He gives 3 to Kyle.

    How many are left?

    $$9 - 3 = \underline{}$$

    $$9 + 3 = \underline{}$$

3. Jess makes 8 .

    Steve makes 1 more than Jess.

    How many does
    Steve make?

    $$8 - 1 = \underline{}$$

    $$8 + 1 = \underline{}$$

4. Julie has 9 .

    She gives 2 to Paul.

    How many does
    she have now?

    $$2 + 9 = \underline{}$$

    $$9 - 2 = \underline{}$$

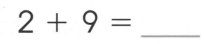
Home Connection Tell your child a word problem. Ask him
or her to decide whether to add or subtract to solve the problem.

two hundred forty-three   **243**

Circle the correct number sentence. Then solve.

1. David has 9 .

   He sells 3.

   How many does he have now?

   $9 - 3 =$ ___ $9 + 3 =$ ___

2. Annie makes 5 .

   Betsy makes 5.

   How many are there altogether?

   $5 - 5 =$ ___ $5 + 5 =$ ___

3. Lisa makes 6 .

   She sells 1.

   How many does she have left?

   $6 - 1 =$ ___ $6 + 1 =$ ___

4. Make your own problem.

   Fill in the ____. Then solve.

   Tanya has ____ .

   She sells ____.

   How many does she have now?

   ____ $+$ ____ $=$ ____   ____ $-$ ____ $=$ ____

© Silver Burdett Ginn Inc. All rights reserved.

Name_____

Complete the addition table.
Tell about the patterns you see.

+	0	1	2	3	4	5	6	7	8	9
0	0	1	2							
1										
2									10	
3					7					
4		5								
5										
6						11				
7										
8										
9				12						

Name_____

Use a .

Circle + or −.

1. Press [ON/C] **5** **3** [=] 2

2. Press [ON/C] **7** **2** [=] 5

3. Press [ON/C] **3** **7** [=] 10

4. Press [ON/C] **9** **9** [=] 0

5. Press [ON/C] **8** **5** [=] 3

6. Press [ON/C] **6** **5** [=] 11

© Silver Burdett Ginn Inc. All rights reserved.

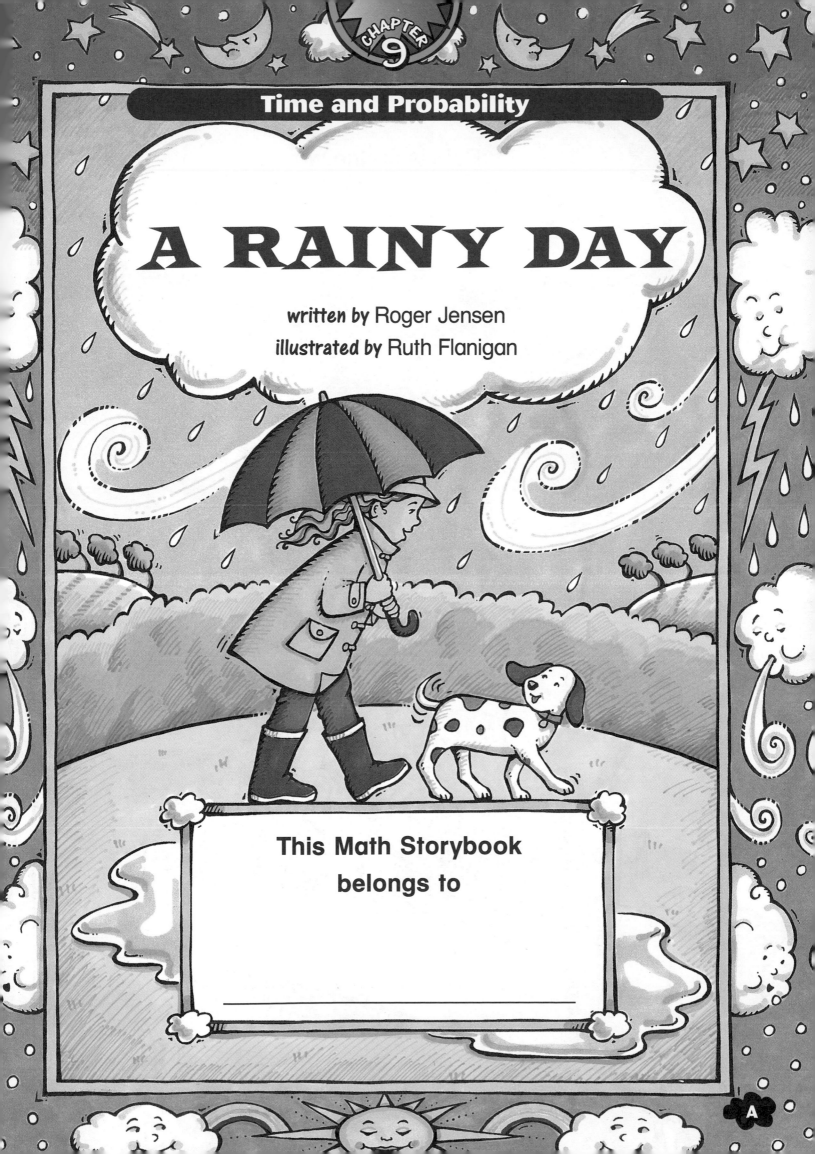

Rain is on the way.
What can I do today?
I'll have pancakes for breakfast.

© Silver Burdett Ginn Inc. All rights reserved.

B

Rain, rain, go away!
I still can't go outside and play.
I'll dress up.

© Silver Burdett Ginn Inc. All rights reserved.

The rain! The rain! It's gone away!
A rainbow has come out today.
Now I can go out and play!

© Silver Burdett Ginn, Inc. All rights reserved.

F

What happened first? What happened last?

3   1   2

Write **1**, **2**, and **3** to show the order.

1.

            3

2.

2   3

3.

3   2   1

Home Connection Discuss the events of the day with your child. Help your child to describe what happened first, next, and last.

two hundred fifty-one   **251**

Make Your Own

What do you do in a day?
Draw pictures to show your day.
Complete each sentence.

1.

First, I _do jumpeng jacks_.

2.

Next, I _do pushup_.

3.

Last, I _go to my nana_.

© Silver Burdett Ginn Inc. All rights reserved.

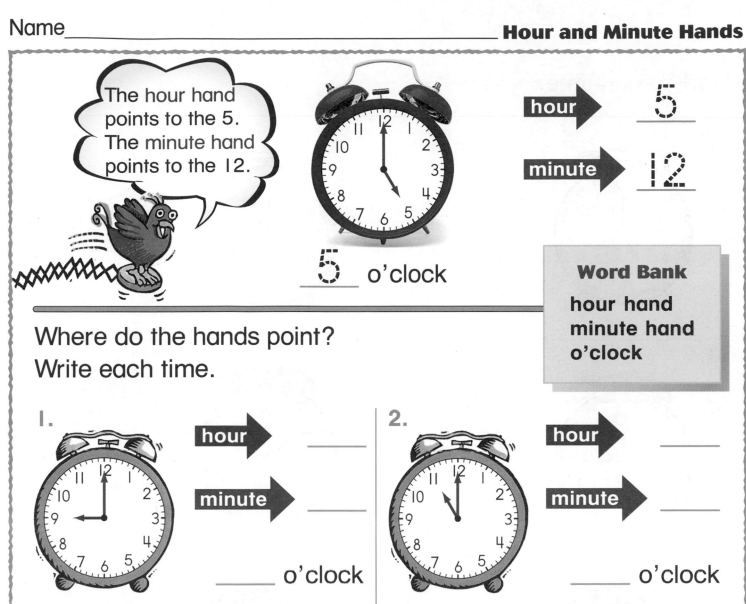

The hour hand points to the 5.
The minute hand points to the 12.

hour ➡ 5

minute ➡ 12

5 o'clock

Word Bank

hour hand
minute hand
o'clock

Where do the hands point?
Write each time.

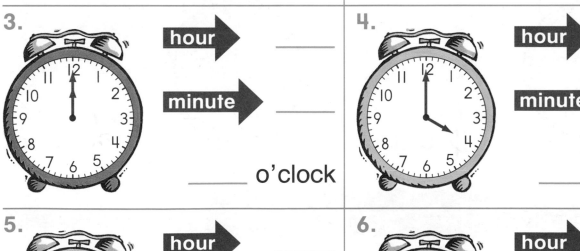

1.
hour ➡ ____
minute ➡ ____
____ o'clock

2.
hour ➡ ____
minute ➡ ____
____ o'clock

3.
hour ➡ ____
minute ➡ ____
____ o'clock

4.
hour ➡ ____
minute ➡ ____
____ o'clock

5.
hour ➡ ____
minute ➡ ____
____ o'clock

6.
hour ➡ ____
minute ➡ ____
____ o'clock

Home Connection Your child is learning about the hour and minute hands on the clock. Use a clock that has hour and minute hands, and discuss what each shows.

two hundred fifty-seven **257**

Write each time.

1.

_7_ o'clock

2.

_1_ o'clock

3.

_3_ o'clock

4.

_10_ o'clock

5.

_6_ o'clock

6.

_9_ o'clock

What Do You Think?

Journal Idea

I think it is easy to tell time when the minute hand is on the 12. Do you agree? Why or why not?

© Silver Burdett Ginn Inc. All rights reserved.

5 o'clock

5:00

Draw the hour hand.
Write each time.

1. 3 o'clock

3:00

2. 6 o'clock

12:00

3. 8 o'clock

12:00

4. 1 o'clock

12:00

5. 11 o'clock

12:00

6. 12 o'clock

12:00

Home Connection Your child is learning to tell time on analog and digital clocks. Help your child to tell the time on both kinds of clocks.

Write the time.
Draw the clock hands.

1.  5:00

_5_ o'clock

2.  10:00

10:00 o'clock

3. 4:00

4:00 o'clock

4. 7:00

7:00 o'clock

Checkpoint

1. Write **1**, **2**, and **3** to show the order.

1

2

3

2. Does it take **more** or **less** than a minute? Circle.

(more)   less

3. Write the time.

9:00

© Silver Burdett Ginn Inc. All rights reserved.

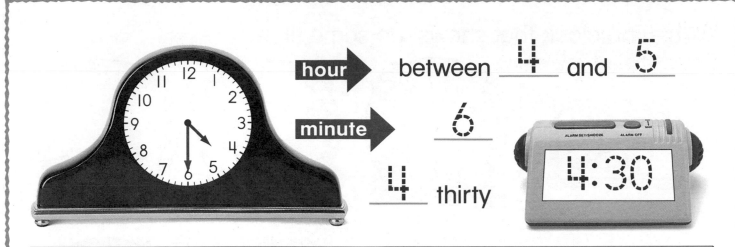

hour ➤ between __4__ and __5__

minute ➤ __6__

__4__ thirty

4:30

___

Where do the hands point?
Tell and write each time.

1.

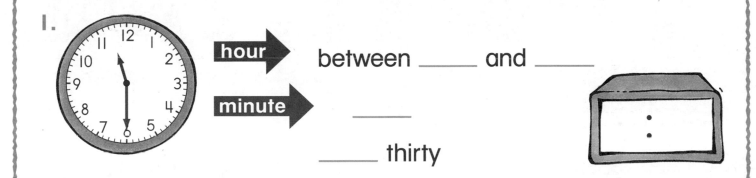

hour ➤ between _____ and _____

minute ➤ _____

_____ thirty

2.

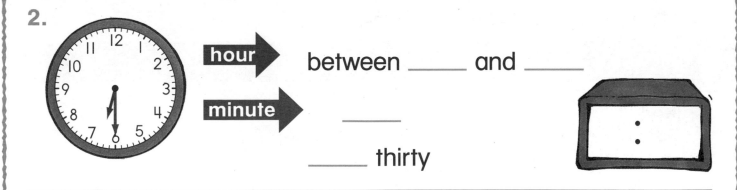

hour ➤ between _____ and _____

minute ➤ _____

_____ thirty

3.

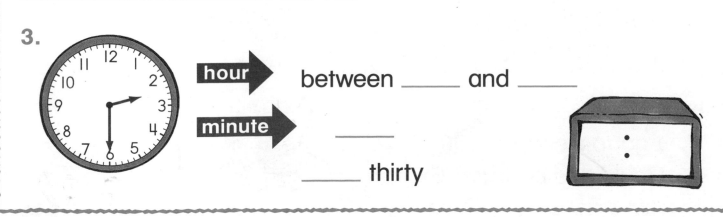

hour ➤ between _____ and _____

minute ➤ _____

_____ thirty

Home Connection Your child is learning to tell time to the half-hour. Use a clock from your house to practice telling time with your child.

Circle the clock that shows the same time.

1.

2.

3.

Problem Solving

Solve.

4. I am meeting Steve at 10:30.
   I get there at 10:00.
   Steve is not there.
   Am I late or early? Explain.

5. I wake up at 7:00.
   I go to sleep at 7:00.
   Could this be true? Explain.

© Silver Burdett Ginn Inc. All rights reserved.

Name_____

Soo Lin starts dance
class at 3:00.
She has class for 1 hour.
What time will dance
class be over?

It is 3:00.
What time will
it be in 1 hour?

 Understand
You need to find what time
it will be 1 hour after 3:00.

 Plan
You can use a clock to act out the time.

 Solve
Start at 3:00. Move the minute hand
around the clock for 1 hour.

Dance class is
over at 4:00

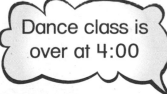 **Look Back**
How does using a clock help you?

Use a clock to act out the time.
Draw the clock hands.

Start	How long?	What time will it be
I. (clock)	 The men paint for 2 hours.	(clock)

Home Connection Have your child write down the start and stop
times for an activity he or she has done. Ask how long the activity took.

two hundred sixty-three **263**

What time will it be?
Use a clock.
Draw the clock hands.

Start	How long?	What time will it be?
1.	Benito bakes for 3 hours.	
2.	Tom works for 2 hours.	
3.	Vicki rides for 1 hour.	
4.	They eat for 30 minutes.	

© Silver Burdett Ginn Inc. All rights reserved.

Name_____
Problem Solving
Reading a Schedule
APPLICATION
Understand
Plan
Look Back
Solve

Morning Schedule

Time	Subject	
9:00	Reading	
10:00	Math	
11:00	Lunch	
11:30	Recess	

Use the schedule.

Circle the correct activity for each time.

Think: The schedule tells when each activity starts.

1.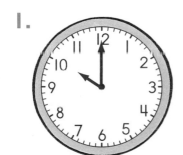

Reading   Math   Lunch

2.

Lunch   Reading   Recess

3.

Recess   Lunch   Math

Home Connection Have your child make a schedule of his or her day. Read the schedule together and discuss the day's events.

Billy's After-School Schedule

Time	Event
3:00	Leave school.
3:30	Have a snack.
4:00	Play.
5:30	Eat dinner.

Use the schedule. Solve.

1. What does Billy do at 4:00?

   _____

   _____

2. What time does Billy eat dinner?

   _____

3. Does Billy have a snack before or after he plays?

   _____

4. What does Billy do before having a snack?

   _____

   _____

5. What do you think Billy does after dinner?

   _____

© Silver Burdett Ginn Inc. All rights reserved.

One side is ● .
One side is ○ .
Which side will it land on?

Use a counter like above.
Toss it a few times.
Will the counter land as shown?
Circle **certain**, **impossible**, or **maybe**.

1.	●	certain	impossible	(maybe)
2.	●	certain	impossible	maybe
3.	○	certain	impossible	maybe
4.	● or ○	certain	impossible	maybe
5.	○ or ●	certain	impossible	maybe

Home Connection Ask your child to think about some events that definitely happen (certain), some events that cannot happen (impossible), and some events that might happen (maybe).

two hundred sixty-nine **269**

Will it happen?

Mark **certain**, **impossible**, or **maybe**.

1. It will rain tomorrow.

☐ certain

☐ impossible

☐ maybe

2. A dog will talk.

☐ certain

☐ impossible

☐ maybe

3. I will get mail today.

☐ certain

☐ impossible

☐ maybe

4. A cat will fly.

☐ certain

☐ impossible

☐ maybe

5. A kangaroo will hop.

☐ certain

☐ impossible

☐ maybe

© Silver Burdett Ginn Inc. All rights reserved.

Name_____ **Tallying Results**

Tallies can help you record how many.

1	2	3	4	5	6
one	two	three	four	five	six
I	II	III	IIII	⊬⊬⊬	⊬⊬⊬ I

Use a 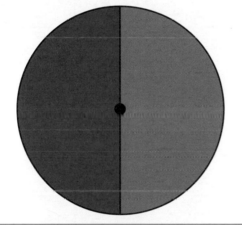 and your pencil to make each spinner.
Spin each 10 times.
Tally to show your results.
Write the totals.

Word Bank
tally

1.

	Tally	Total
Red		
Blue		

2.

	Tally	Total
Red		
Blue		

3. Did both spinners give you the same results?
Tell why or why not.

Home Connection Your child is learning that some events are more likely to happen than others. Encourage your child to talk about the results of the experiments on this page.

Use a and your pencil to make each spinner.
Spin each 10 times.
Tally to show your results.
Write the totals.

1.

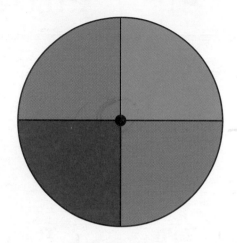

	Tally	Total
Red		
Blue		
Green		

2.

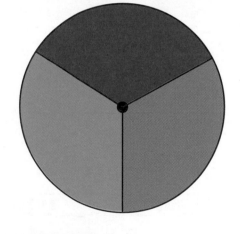

	Tally	Total
Red		
Blue		
Green		

Critical Thinking Corner

Logical Thinking   Journal Idea

Which spinner would be more
likely to land on blue? Tell why.

© Silver Burdett Ginn Inc. All rights reserved.

Where do the hands point?
Write the time.

1.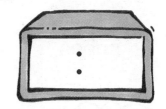

hour ➤ between _____ and _____

minute ➤ _____

_____ thirty

Will it happen?
Circle **certain**, **impossible**, or **maybe**.

2.

The ice cream will melt.

certain   impossible   maybe

3.

A fish will play ball.

certain   impossible   maybe

What time will it be?
Draw the clock hands.

Start	How long?	What time will it be?
4.	Zach naps for 2 hours.	

Name_____

What You Need

cubes

2-color counter

clock

START

7:00

7:30 → Short Cut → 10:00 10:30 11:00

11:30   9:30 9:00 8:30 8:00

Pick a cube.
Take turns with a partner.
Toss a 2-color counter.
Move your cube 30 minutes for red.
Move 1 hour for yellow.
Name the time on that space.
Show it on the clock.
The first person to reach the end wins.

12:00

12:30

1:00

1:30   2:00   2:30   3:00   3:30

Short Cut

4:00

END   6:30   6:00   5:30   5:00   4:30

© Silver Burdett Ginn Inc. All rights reserved.

1. Write **1**, **2**, and **3** to show the order.

_____ _____ _____

About how long does each take?
Circle **minutes** or **hours**.

2. Brush your teeth.

minutes   hours

3. Play baseball.

minutes   hours

Where do the hands point?
Write the time.

4.

hour ➡ between _____ and _____

minute ➡ _____

_____ thirty

Use the schedule.
Circle the correct activity for each time.

5.

Games   Swimming   Lunch

6.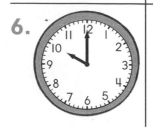

Crafts   Swimming   Lunch

Camp Schedule

Time	Activity
10:00	Swimming
11:00	Crafts
12:00	Lunch
1:00	Games

Name_____

What You Need

clock

crayons

Show the time on your clock.
Draw the clock hands.
Draw a picture of something
you might do at this time.

1. 4 o'clock		
2. 11:30		
3. 9:00		

Where would the clock hands point for 3 thirty?

 For Your Portfolio
You might put this page in your portfolio.

© Silver Burdett Ginn Inc. All rights reserved.

Name_____

Count by 5s to find the time.

_55_ _60_ _5_

_50_ _10_

_45_ _15_

_40_ _20_

_35_ _25_

_30_

_10_ minutes after _3_

What time is it? Write the numbers.

1.

_20_ minutes after 11

2.

_40_ minutes after 4

3.

_15_ minutes after 9

4.

_50_ minutes after 12

How many times will the spinner land on 1 ?

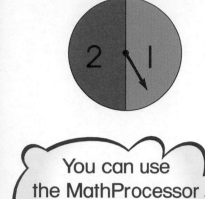

You can use the MathProcessor to find out.

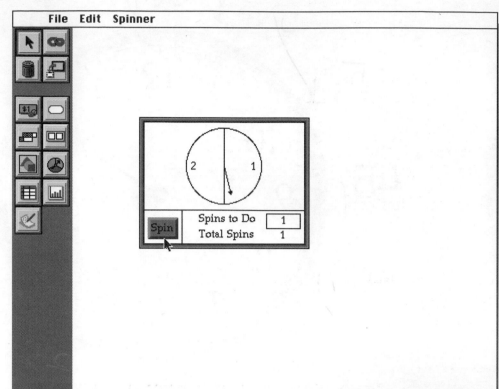

Take turns with a partner.

1 Click on the **spinner button** to show a spinner.

2 Circle the number you think will be spun more.

1 2

3 Click on the word .
Spin 20 times.

4 Tally the number for each spin.
Write the totals.

Compare your results with those of your classmates.

	Tally	Total
1		
2		

© Silver Burdett Ginn Inc. All rights reserved.

Name_____

Fill in the ◯ for the correct answer.

1. Find how many.

◯ 7   ◯ 6   ● 9   ◯ 10

2. Which number comes between?

9, ____, 11

◯ 8   ◯ 12   ◯ 5   ● 10

Add or subtract.

3. 9
+ 3

◯ 11
● 12
◯ 6
◯ 7

4. 7
− 4

◯ 9
◯ 11
● 3
◯ 0

5. 5
− 5

◯ 10
◯ 7
● 0
◯ 11

6. 6
+ 5

◯ 10
◯ 1
● 11
◯ 12

7. 8
− 3

◯ 4
◯ 12
◯ 11
● 5

8. 4
+ 2

● 6
◯ 2
◯ 8
◯ 10

9. 4
+ 7

● 11
◯ 12
◯ 9
◯ 8

10. 12
− 6

◯ 4
◯ 10
● 6
◯ 7

11. 11
− 5

◯ 5
◯ 12
◯ 7
● 6

12. Choose the correct number sentence.

◯ 5 + 3 = 8   ● 5 − 2 = 3
◯ 7 + 2 = 9   ◯ 7 − 5 = 2

13. Which object has the same shape?

◯　◯　◯　◯

14. What part is blue?

◯ $\frac{1}{3}$　◯ $\frac{1}{2}$　◯ $\frac{1}{4}$

15. What number comes before?

_____ , 98, 99

◯　◯　◯　◯

89　97　100　96

16. How many are there?

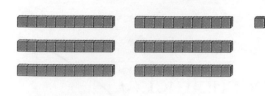

◯　◯　◯　◯

71　62　51　80

17. What can you buy?

47¢　40¢　44¢

◯　◯　◯

18. What time is it?

◯ 7:00
◯ 8:30
◯ 8:00
◯ 12:00

19. What time is it?

◯ 1:00
◯ 4:00
◯ 2:00
◯ 9:00

20. What time will it be in 1 hour?

4:30

◯　◯　◯

Chapter 9 Cumulative Review

© Silver Burdett Ginn Inc. All rights reserved.

Measurement

HOW DO YOU MEASURE A PIG?

written by Teri Jones

illustrated by Rosanne Litzinger

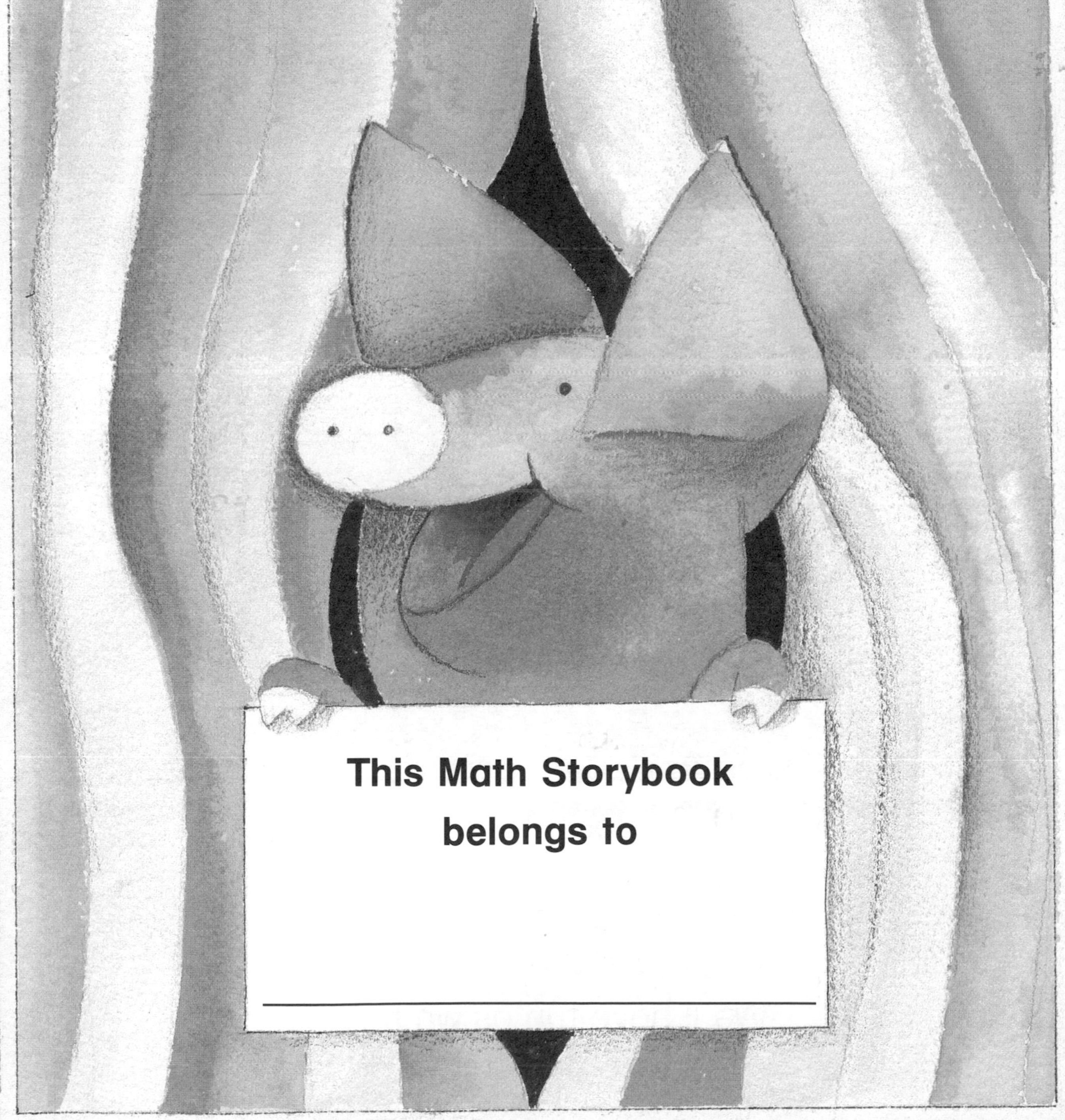

This Math Storybook

belongs to

_____

Come to the pig fair and win a prize.
Pigs of all sizes are welcome.
We'll have fun as we find out
how to measure a pig!

© Silver Burdett Ginn Inc. All rights reserved.

Slim is the winner of a prize.
He's the tallest pig of all!
Slim is 30 inches from head to foot.
That's how you measure a pig.

Oink is the winner of a prize.
She's the longest pig of all!
Oink is 36 inches from snout to tail.
That's how you measure a pig.

Big Bert is the winner of a prize.
He's the heaviest pig of all!
Big Bert weighs 300 pounds.
That's how you measure a pig.

Little Gert is the winner of a prize.
She is the nicest pig of all!
She measures up in a special way.
Is that how you measure a pig?

© Silver Burdett Ginn Inc. All rights reserved.

How many ways can you measure Little Gert?
Use a ruler.
Tell what you find.

INTERNET ACTIVITY

www.sbgmath.com

G

A Note to the Family

**Here are some learning ideas
you can share with your child.**

Enjoy *How Do You Measure a Pig?* Together

- Read the story aloud together. Talk about the prize each pig won.

- On the last page of the story, talk about different ways a pig could be measured, such as its length from snout to tail or its height from head to foot. Work with your child to measure the parts of Little Gert with a ruler. Write down each part and the measurement.

At-Home Activities

- Using a tape measure, a ruler, and/or a yardstick, measure different objects in your home. For example, you could measure the height of a table, the height of a glass, the length of a shoe, and the width of a window. You might also measure around a lamp or other circular objects. Help your child compare measurements to decide what items are the tallest, longest, and widest.

- In the kitchen, select several empty containers and have your child guess how many 8-oz cups of water each container will hold. Then use a measuring cup to see how much water is needed to fill each container. Then compare the guesses with the actual amounts.

Read More About It!

To read more about measurement with your child, look for these books in your local library.

- *The Carrot Seed* by Ruth Krauss
  (HarperCollins Children's Books, 1989)

- *Farmer Mack Measures His Pig* by Tony Johnston
  (HarperCollins Children's Books, 1986)

- *How Big Is a Foot?* by Rolf Myller (Dell, 1991)

- *How to Weigh an Elephant* by Bob Barner (Bantam, 1995)

Visit Our Web Site!

INTERNET ACTIVITY
www.sbgmath.com

© Silver Burdett Ginn Inc. All rights reserved.

Name_____ **Understanding Length and Height**

Are you shorter or taller
than the real object?
Compare to find out.
Circle **shorter** or **taller**.

Word Bank

shorter
taller
longer

1.

shorter

(taller)

trash can

2.

(shorter)

taller

door

3.

(shorter)

taller

closet

4.

shorter

(taller)

desk

5.

shorter

(taller)

watering can

6.

shorter

(taller)

bookshelf

Home Connection Children are learning to compare
lengths and heights of objects. Encourage your child to compare
objects at home, using the words "shorter," "longer," and "taller."

two hundred eighty-one   **281**

Circle the longer object.

Put an **X** on the shorter object.

1.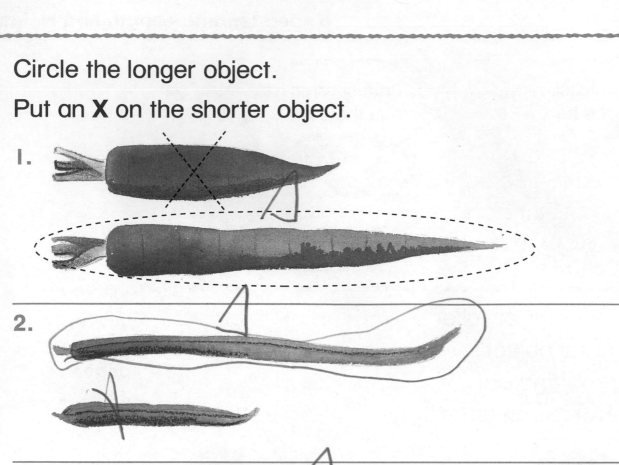

2.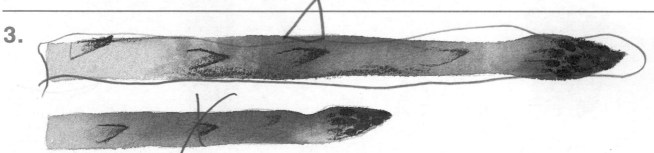

3.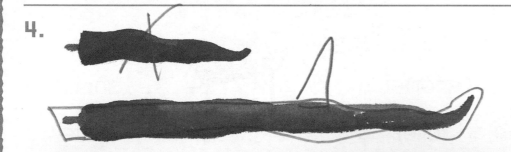

4.

© Silver Burdett Ginn Inc. All rights reserved.

What Do You Think?

Journal Idea

 Look at all the objects on this page.
Which one is the longest?
Tell how you know.

Name_____

Problem Solving
Guess and Check

STRATEGY

Understand
Plan
Look Back
Solve

About how many cubes long is the worm?

 Understand
You need to find out how many cubes fit along the length of the worm.

 Plan
You can guess the number of cubes. Then measure with cubes to check.

 Solve

I think the worm is about 4 cubes long.

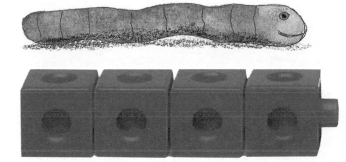

The worm is about 4 cubes long.

 Look Back
Did you guess the correct number?

About how long is the bug?
Guess. Then measure with cubes.

 1.

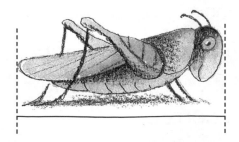

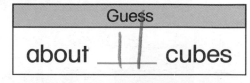

Guess
about __11__ cubes

Measure
about _____ cubes

 Home Connection Ask your child to guess the length of objects at home in paper clips, then measure to check.

two hundred eighty-three **283**

About how many cubes long is each bug?
Guess and then measure.

1.

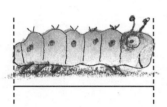

Guess
about _____ cubes

Measure
about _____ cubes

2.

Guess
about _____ cubes

Measure
about _____ cubes

3. Draw your own bug.

Make Your Own

Guess
about _____ cubes

Measure
about _____ cubes

Critical Thinking Corner

Visual Thinking **Journal Idea**

Kelly guesses the pencil is about 9 cubes long.
Peg guesses it is about 2 crayons long.
How can both girls be correct?

The pencil is about 5 inches long.

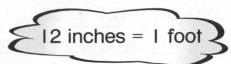

12 inches = 1 foot

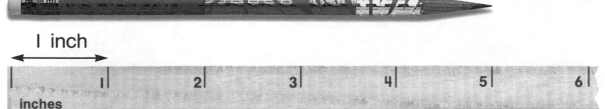

1 inch

inches

About how long is the real object?
Use an inch ruler to measure.

Word Bank

inch
foot

1. crayon

about _____ inches

2. paper clip

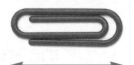

about _____ inches

3. 3 cubes

about _____ inches

4. eraser

about _____ inches

5. marker

about _____ inches

6. book

about _____ inches

Home Connection Children are learning to measure in inches. Ask your child to use a ruler to measure common items at home, such as spoons, toys, pencils, and books.

Use an inch ruler.
Write how many inches long or tall.

1.

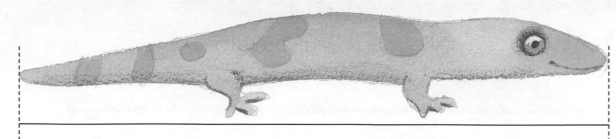

about   6   inches long

2.

about _____ inches long

3.

about _____ inches tall

4.

about _____ inch tall

5. Draw your own object.
About how long is it?
About how tall is it?

about _____ inches long

about _____ inches tall

© Silver Burdett Ginn Inc. All rights reserved.

Name_____ **Centimeters**

About how long is the mouse's tail?

10 centimeters = 1 decimeter

1 centimeter

←→

| 1 | 2 | 3 | 4 | 5 | 6 | 7 | 8 | 9 | 10 | 11 | 12 |
centimeters

Work with a partner.
Use a centimeter ruler to measure.

Word Bank

centimeter
decimeter

1. Your ear
   about _____
   centimeters

2. Your thumb
   about _____
   centimeters

3. Your hand
   about _____
   centimeters

4. Your forearm
   about _____
   centimeters

5. Your foot
   about _____
   centimeters

Home Connection Invite your child to find things at home that are about 10 centimeters long. Help your child check the measurements with a centimeter ruler.

two hundred eighty-seven   **287**

Use a centimeter ruler to measure.

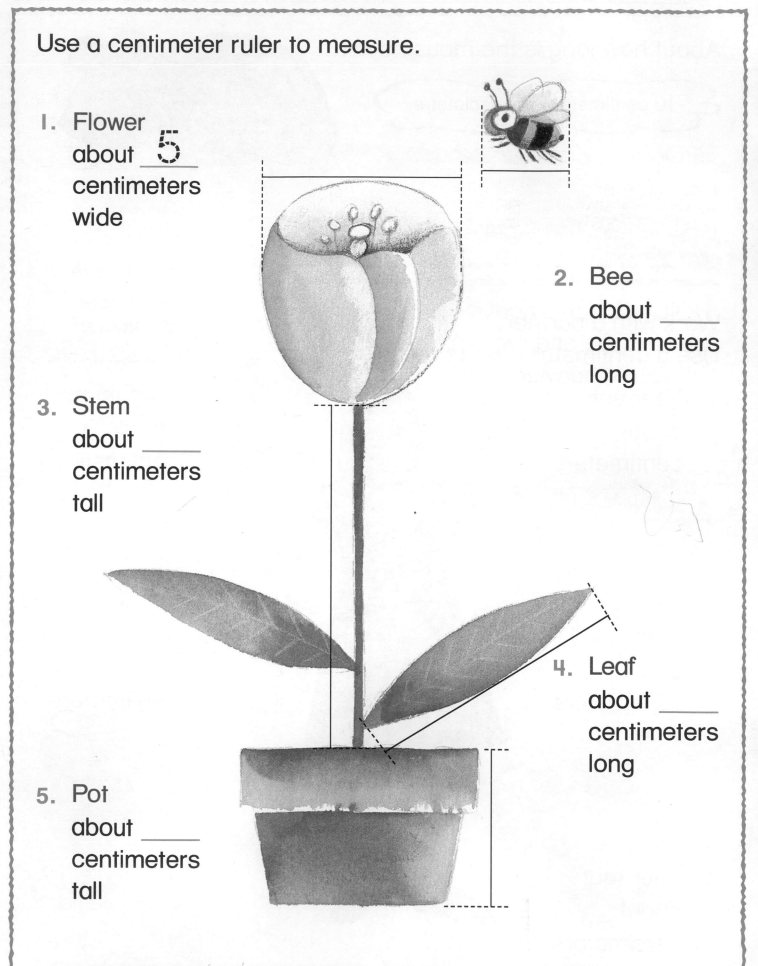

1. Flower about __5__ centimeters wide

2. Bee about ____ centimeters long

3. Stem about ____ centimeters tall

4. Leaf about ____ centimeters long

5. Pot about ____ centimeters tall

© Silver Burdett Ginn Inc. All rights reserved.

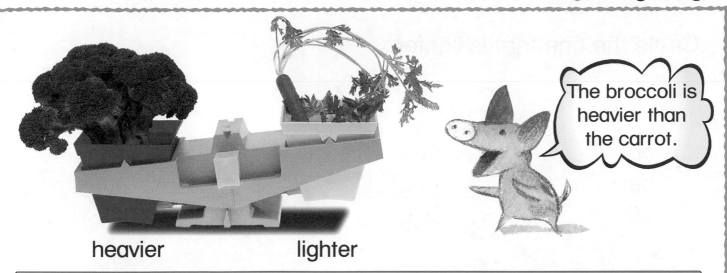

heavier   lighter

The broccoli is heavier than the carrot.

Which object is heavier?
Use a scale and real objects.
Circle the heavier object.

Word Bank
heavier
lighter

I.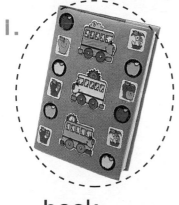

book   tape

2.

ruler   crayons

3.

eraser   chalk

4.

calculator   paint

 Home Connection Your child is learning how to compare the weight of objects. Encourage your child to pick up different objects in each hand and tell which is heavier and which is lighter.

two hundred eighty-nine   **289**

Circle the one that is lighter.

1.

2.

3.

4.

© Silver Burdett Ginn Inc. All rights reserved.

What Do You Think?

Journal Idea

I think that big objects are not always heavier than small objects.
What do you think? Explain.

less than 1 pound   about 1 pound   more than 1 pound

Does each weigh **more** or **less** than 1 pound?
Circle **more** or **less**.

Word Bank
pound

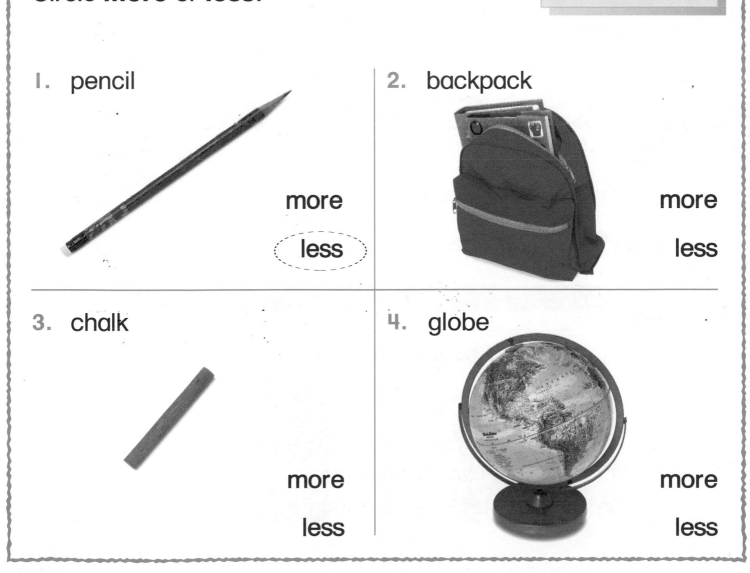

1. pencil

more

(less)

2. backpack

more

less

3. chalk

more

less

4. globe

more

less

Circle the things that weigh
less than 1 pound.

Checkpoint

1. Circle the longer object.

2. Circle the heavier object. | 3. Circle the lighter object.

© Silver Burdett Ginn Inc. All rights reserved.

 =

2 cups fill 1 pint.   2 pints fill 1 quart.

How many can you fill?
Circle to show how many.

Word Bank
cup
pint
quart

1.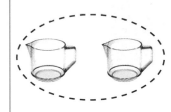

2.

3.

4.

Home Connection Your child is learning about cups, pints, and quarts. On a trip to the supermarket, have your child identify containers and compare the quantities each holds.

two hundred ninety-seven   **297**

Remember,
2 cups fill 1 pint.
2 pints fill 1 quart.

Circle the two that hold
the same amount.

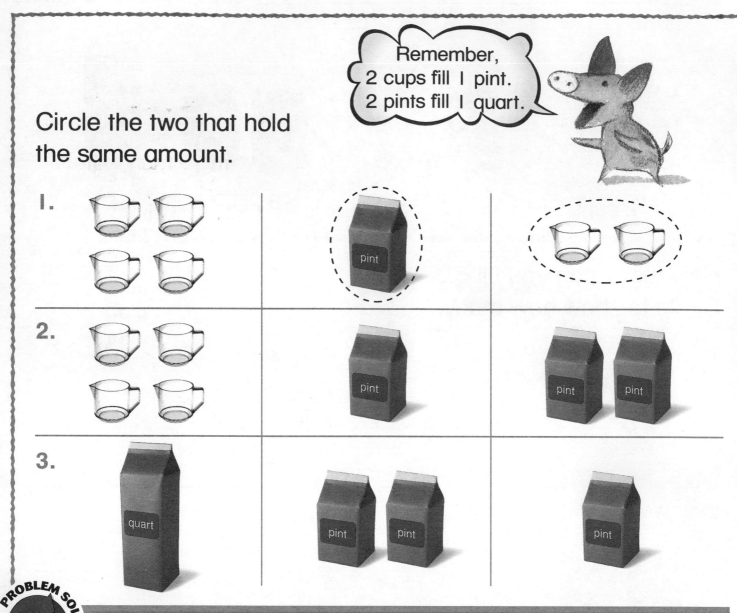

1.

2.

3.

Problem Solving

4. Is there enough juice to make the fruit punch?
Circle **yes** or **no**.
Tell why or why not.

Fruit Punch

1 cup orange juice

1 quart pineapple juice

1 pint cranberry juice

yes   no

© Silver Burdett Ginn Inc. All rights reserved.

less than 1 liter

1 liter

more than 1 liter

Word Bank
liter

Circle the things that hold more than 1 liter.

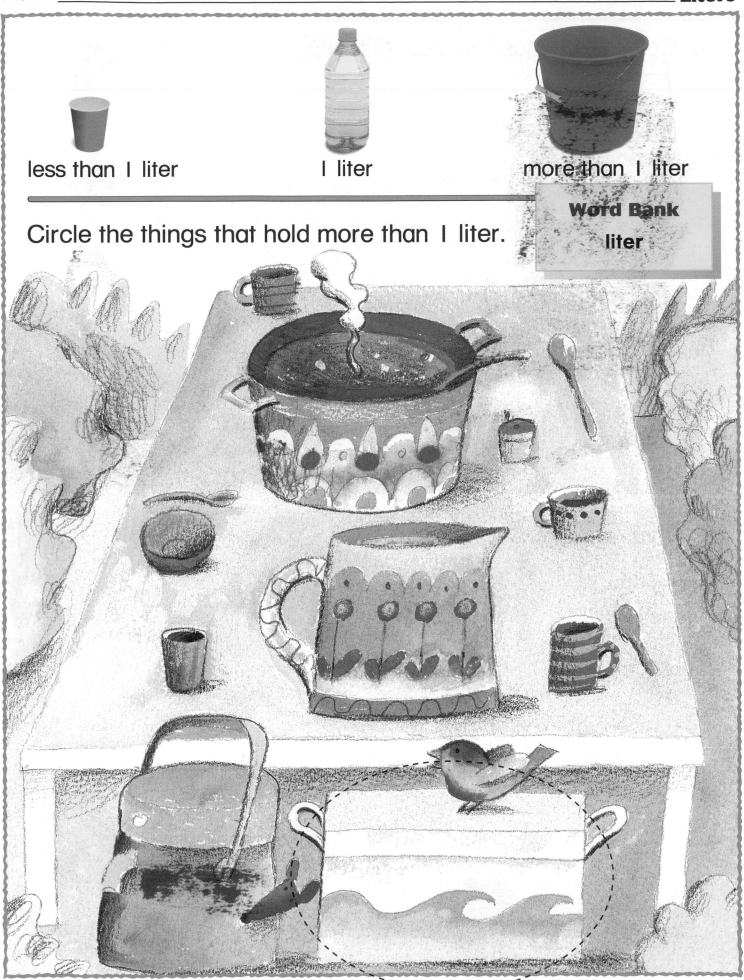

Home Connection Children are learning about liters. Display a 1-liter bottle at home and help your child find containers that hold more than, less than, and about 1 liter.

1. Color the things that hold less than 1 liter.

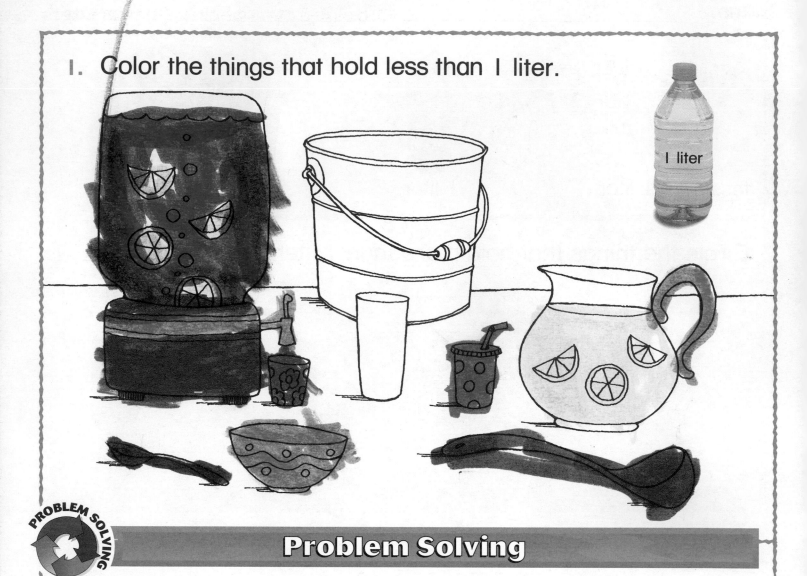

I liter

PROBLEM SOLVING

Problem Solving

Estimation

Solve.

2. Each jar holds 4 liters.
   About how many more liters do
   you need to fill each jar?

about _____ liters

about _____ liters

© Silver Burdett Ginn Inc. All rights reserved.

Name_____

APPLICATION
Understand
Plan
Solve
Look Back

Problem Solving
Choosing Reasonable Answers

Use the right tool to measure.
Think: What do you need to find out?

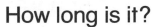

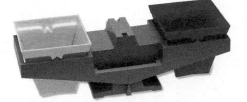

How long is it?   How much does it hold?   How heavy is it?

Circle the tool you would use.

I.   How long is it?

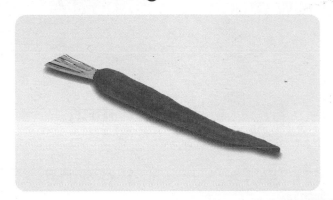

2.   How heavy is it?

3.   How much does it hold?

4.   How tall is it?

Home Connection Invite your child to name things in your home
that can be measured with a ruler, a measuring cup, and a scale.

three hundred one   **301**

Circle the correct measurement.

1. How long is it?

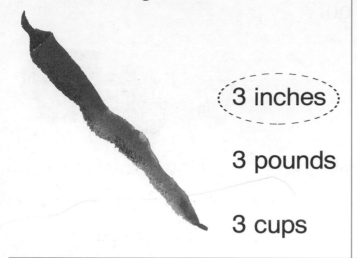

(3 inches)

3 pounds

3 cups

2. How much does it hold?

1 inch

1 pound

1 quart

3. How heavy is it?

5 inches

5 pounds

5 pints

4. How much does it hold?

1 inch

1 pound

1 cup

5. How tall is it?

2 inches

2 pounds

2 cups

6. How heavy is it?

4 inches

4 pounds

4 cups

© Silver Burdett Ginn Inc. All rights reserved.

Name_____

Does it weigh **more** or **less**
than 1 kilogram?
Circle **more** or **less**.

1.

2.

(less)   more

less   (more)

Circle the container that holds the most.
Order the containers from most to least.

3.

Circle the containers that hold less than 1 liter.

4.

How long is it?
Circle the tool you would use.

5.

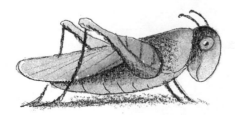   

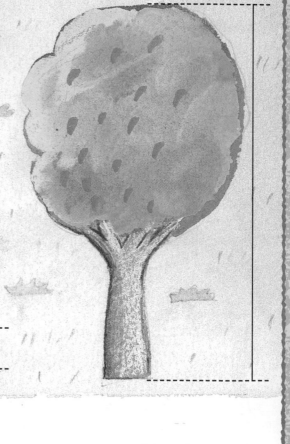

Tiny Town Country Fair

Use a centimeter ruler to measure.

1. The 🚐 is about __9__ centimeters long.

2. The 🌳 is about _____ centimeters tall.

3. The 🦆 is about _____ centimeters tall.

4. The 🐷 is about _____ centimeters long.

5. The 🐥 is about _____ centimeter tall.

© Silver Burdett Ginn Inc. All rights reserved.

About how long is each one?
Circle the better answer.

1.

2.

2 inches   6 inches

3 centimeters   5 centimeters

Does it weigh more or less
than 1 pound?
Circle **more** or **less**.

3.

more
less

Does it weigh more or less
than 1 kilogram?
Circle **more** or **less**.

4.

more
less

How many cups can you fill?
Circle to show how many.

5.

pint

6.

quart

Circle the containers that hold
more than 1 liter.

7.

How much does it hold?
Circle the tool you would use.

8.

Name_____ **Performance Assessment**

Pick an object. Draw it.
Measure to tell about it.

[ ]

1. It weighs more than _____.

2. It weighs less than _____.

3. It is about _____ tall.

4. It is about _____ long.

5. What tools did you use to measure?

_____

_____

For Your Portfolio
You might put this page in your portfolio.

© Silver Burdett Ginn Inc. All rights reserved.

90° F

90 degrees

20° F

20 degrees

Circle the picture that shows each temperature.

1. 80° F

2. 60° F

3. 30° F

About how many cubes
will cover a workspace?

You can use the
MathProcessor
to find out.

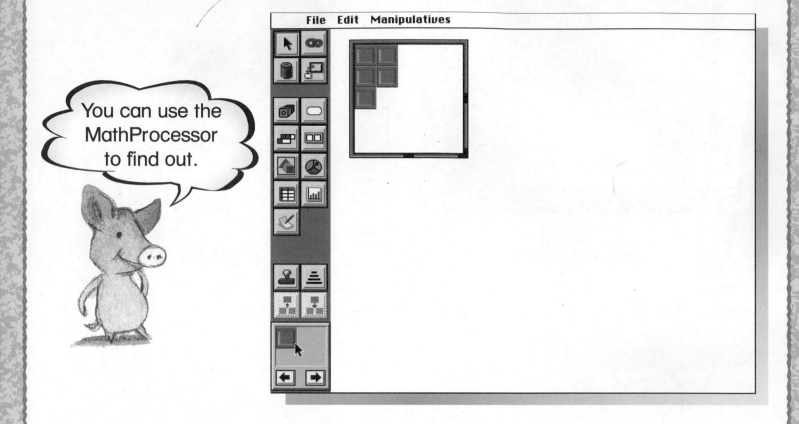

Take turns with a partner.

1 Click on the **cube button** to show a workspace.

2 Click on the **arrow** to pick a cube color.

3 Click on the **cube** 5 times to show 5 cubes. Guess how many cubes will cover the workspace.

4 Click on the **cube** to cover the workspace. Stop to guess again. Then count.

Change the size of the workspace.
How many cubes cover it now?

© Silver Burdett Ginn Inc. All rights reserved.

Addition and Subtraction to 18

Look Who's Here!

written by Roxane Fox

illustrated by Rose Mary Berlin

This Math Storybook

belongs to

_____

A

It is springtime in the desert.
Many animals wake up from a long winter rest.
Look who's here!

There are 10 iguanas.
7 hurry away.
How many iguanas will be left?

© Silver Burdett Ginn Inc. All rights reserved

B

The desert air is hot and dry.
Animals look for water.
Look who's here!

9 rabbits drink.
Here come 9 quails.
How many animals are there in all?

In springtime the cactuses bloom.
Many animals walk near the cactuses.
Look who's here!

There are 13 Gila monsters.
4 walk away.
How many Gila monsters will be left?

© Silver Burdett Ginn Inc. All rights reserved.

The air gets cool when the sun goes down.
This is when some animals look for food.
Look who's here!

4 coyotes watch their pups.
8 pups play.
How many coyotes are there in all?

It is nighttime in the desert.
Some animals come out at night.
Look who's here!

17 bats hunt for food.
9 fly back to their cave.
How many bats will be left?

© Silver Burdett Ginn Inc. All rights reserved.

F

Color the desert animals.
What if there were 4 more?
What if there were 5 fewer?
Tell how many there will be.

INTERNET ACTIVITY
www.sbgmath.com

G

A Note to the Family

Here are some learning ideas you can share with your child.

Enjoy *Look Who's Here!* Together

- Read each page of the story with your child. Ask whether he or she needs to add or subtract in order to find the answer to the question on each page. Help your child write addition or subtraction sentences to find how many there are in all or how many are left.

    For example: 4 big coyotes and 8 little coyotes are 12 in all
    $$4 + 8 = 12$$

- Ask your child to tell how many animals are on the last page of the story. Encourage him or her to tell number stories about more animals coming along or some going away.

At-Home Activity

- Use peanuts, raisins, grapes, or any other small snack food. To practice addition, give your child 2 groups of snacks and have him or her tell you an addition sentence that shows how many there are in all. To practice subtraction, begin with a single group and tell your child that she or he may eat a specified number. Before he or she eats, ask your child to say a subtraction sentence that describes how many will be left.

Read More About It!

To read more stories about the desert or addition and subtraction, look for these books in your local library.

- *Desert Giant: The World of the Saguaro Cactus* by Barbara Bash (Sierra Club Books/Little, Brown, 1989)

- *Caps for Sale* by Esphyr Slobodkina (HarperCollins, 1987)

- *Eat Up, Gemma* by Sarah Hayes (Harcourt Brace, 1993)

Visit Our Web Site!

INTERNET ACTIVITY
www.sbgmath.com

I can make a double.
I start with 4 cubes.
Then I add 4 more.

4 + 4 = 8

Use two colors of cubes and Workmat 4.
Show each number. Then show the double.
Complete the addition sentence.

1. Show 3.

3 + 3 = 6

2. Show 5.

5 + 5 = 10

3. Show 2.

2 + 2 = 4

4. Show 7.

7 + 1 = 8

5. Show 6.

6 + 1 = 7

6. Show 9.

9 + 1 = 10

7. Show 8.

8 + 2 = 10

8. Show 1.

1 + 1 = 2

Home Connection Use buttons or other household items to practice doubles with your child.

three hundred nine **309**

Add. Circle the doubles.
Use cubes if you like.

1. $(2 + 2 = \underline{4})$ $7 + 3 = \underline{10}$ $6 + 6 = \underline{10}$

2. $7 + 7 = \underline{10}$ $3 + 9 = \underline{13}$ $8 + 8 = \underline{10}$

3.
$$\begin{array}{r} 8 \\ +\ 2 \\ \hline 10 \end{array} \qquad \begin{array}{r} 5 \\ +\ 4 \\ \hline 9 \end{array} \qquad \begin{array}{r} 0 \\ +\ 0 \\ \hline 0 \end{array} \qquad \begin{array}{r} 1 \\ +\ 1 \\ \hline 2 \end{array} \qquad \begin{array}{r} 2 \\ +\ 6 \\ \hline 8 \end{array} \qquad \begin{array}{r} 5 \\ +\ 5 \\ \hline 10 \end{array}$$

4.
$$\begin{array}{r} 3 \\ +\ 3 \\ \hline 6 \end{array} \qquad \begin{array}{r} 4 \\ +\ 8 \\ \hline 10 \end{array} \qquad \begin{array}{r} 7 \\ +\ 1 \\ \hline 8 \end{array} \qquad \begin{array}{r} 4 \\ +\ 4 \\ \hline 8 \end{array} \qquad \begin{array}{r} 5 \\ +\ 6 \\ \hline 10 \end{array} \qquad \begin{array}{r} 6 \\ +\ 4 \\ \hline 10 \end{array}$$

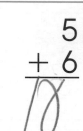 

Problem Solving

Solve.

5. Clara has the same number of red and
blue blocks. She has 16 blocks altogether.
How many blocks does she have?

   _____ red   _____ blue

6. What if Clara had 2 more red than blue blocks?
How many blocks would she have?

   _____ red   _____ blue

© Silver Burdett Ginn Inc. All rights reserved.

Name_____

Subtraction is the opposite of addition.

Use two colors of counters and Workmat 4.
Show each number.
Add. Then subtract.

1. Start with 6. Add 4.

    $6 + 4 = 10$

    Take away 4 to subtract.

    $10 - 4 = 6$

2. Start with 7. Add 6.

    ___ + ___ = ___

    Take away 6 to subtract.

    ___ − ___ = ___

3. Start with 8. Add 8.

    ___ + ___ = ___

    Take away 8 to subtract.

    ___ − ___ = ___

4. Start with 6. Add 9.

    ___ + ___ = ___

    Take away 9 to subtract.

    ___ − ___ = ___

Home Connection Choose an addition fact. Ask your child he or she found other household items to show the fact and the fact. Then write both number sentences.

three hundred twenty-three **323**

Use two colors of counters and Workmat 4.
Show each number. Add. Then subtract.

	Add	Subtract
1. [4] [9]	$4 + 9 = 13$	$13 - 9 = 4$
2. [5] [8]	___ + ___ = ___	___ − ___ = ___
3. [9] [9]	___ + ___ = ___	___ − ___ = ___
4. [7] [8]	___ + ___ = ___	___ − ___ = ___
5. [5] [9]	___ + ___ = ___	___ − ___ = ___

Problem Solving

Solve.

6. The sum of two numbers is 8.
The difference of the numbers is 2.
What are the numbers? _____ and _____

© Silver Burdett Ginn Inc. All rights reserved.

$7 + 5 = \underline{12}$ $12 - 5 = \underline{7}$

$5 + 7 = \underline{12}$ $12 - 7 = \underline{5}$

Every fact has the same numbers. This must be a fact family.

Add or subtract.
Write the numbers for each fact family.

1.

     14   8   6

$8 + 6 = \underline{}$ $14 - 6 = \underline{}$

$6 + 8 = \underline{}$ $14 - 8 = \underline{}$

2.

     13   6   7

$6 + 7 = \underline{}$ $13 - 7 = \underline{}$

$7 + 6 = \underline{}$ $13 - 6 = \underline{}$

3.

     16   9   7

$9 + 7 = \underline{}$ $16 - 7 = \underline{}$

$7 + 9 = \underline{}$ $16 - 9 = \underline{}$

4.

     13   8   5

$8 + 5 = \underline{}$ $13 - 5 = \underline{}$

$5 + 8 = \underline{}$ $13 - 8 = \underline{}$

Home Connection Fact families are number facts that use the same numbers. Ask your child to write number sentences for a fact family like 3, 9, and 12.

three hundred twenty-seven   **327**

Add and subtract.
Write the numbers for each fact family.

1.
$3 + 9 = 12$ $12 - 9 = 3$
$9 + 3 = 12$ $12 - 3 = 9$

2.
$9 + 4 = \underline{\quad}$ $13 - 4 = \underline{\quad}$
$4 + 9 = \underline{\quad}$ $13 - 9 = \underline{\quad}$

3.
$7 + 8 = \underline{\quad}$ $15 - 8 = \underline{\quad}$
$8 + 7 = \underline{\quad}$ $15 - 7 = \underline{\quad}$

4.
$9 + 8 = \underline{\quad}$ $17 - 8 = \underline{\quad}$
$8 + 9 = \underline{\quad}$ $17 - 9 = \underline{\quad}$

5.
$5 + 9 = \underline{\quad}$ $14 - 9 = \underline{\quad}$
$9 + 5 = \underline{\quad}$ $14 - 5 = \underline{\quad}$

6. Make your own fact family.
Write the number sentences.

$\underline{\quad} + \underline{\quad} = \underline{\quad}$ $\underline{\quad} - \underline{\quad} = \underline{\quad}$

$\underline{\quad} + \underline{\quad} = \underline{\quad}$ $\underline{\quad} - \underline{\quad} = \underline{\quad}$

© Silver Burdett Ginn Inc. All rights reserved.

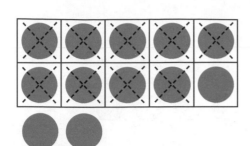
$$\begin{array}{r} 12 \\ -\ \ 9 \\ \hline 3 \end{array}$$

There is 1 in the ten-frame and 2 extra. So 12 − 9 = 3.

Cross out to subtract.
Use counters and Workmat 2 if you like.

1. 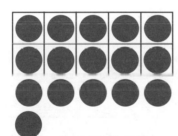 $$\begin{array}{r} 15 \\ -\ \ 8 \\ \hline \end{array}$$

2. 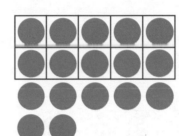 $$\begin{array}{r} 17 \\ -\ \ 9 \\ \hline \end{array}$$

3. 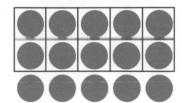 $$\begin{array}{r} 16 \\ -\ \ 9 \\ \hline \end{array}$$

4. 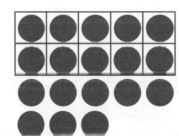 $$\begin{array}{r} 18 \\ -\ \ 9 \\ \hline \end{array}$$

5.  $$\begin{array}{r} 11 \\ -\ \ 8 \\ \hline \end{array}$$

6. 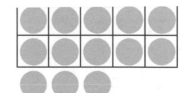 $$\begin{array}{r} 13 \\ -\ \ 8 \\ \hline \end{array}$$

7. 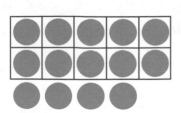 $$\begin{array}{r} 14 \\ -\ \ 8 \\ \hline \end{array}$$

8. 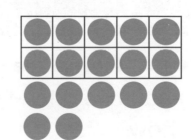 $$\begin{array}{r} 17 \\ -\ \ 8 \\ \hline \end{array}$$

Home Connection Have your child use pennies and a hand-drawn ten-frame to practice using 10 to subtract 8 or 9.

Cross out to subtract.

1.
$$\begin{array}{r} 12 \\ -\ 9 \\ \hline 3 \end{array}$$

2.
$$\begin{array}{r} 15 \\ -\ 9 \\ \hline \end{array}$$

3.
$$\begin{array}{r} 16 \\ -\ 8 \\ \hline \end{array}$$

4.
$$\begin{array}{r} 13 \\ -\ 9 \\ \hline \end{array}$$

5.
$$\begin{array}{r} 14 \\ -\ 9 \\ \hline \end{array}$$

6.
$$\begin{array}{r} 15 \\ -\ 8 \\ \hline \end{array}$$

7.
$$\begin{array}{r} 14 \\ -\ 8 \\ \hline \end{array}$$

8.
$$\begin{array}{r} 16 \\ -\ 9 \\ \hline \end{array}$$

Critical Thinking Corner

Number Sense **Journal Idea**

 You can use a ten-frame to add or subtract.
Tell how.

© Silver Burdett Ginn Inc. All rights reserved.

You can subtract in many ways.

$$\begin{array}{r} 12 \\ -\ 9 \\ \hline 3 \end{array}$$ Think addition. $3 + 9 = 12$

$$\begin{array}{r} 16 \\ -\ 8 \\ \hline 8 \end{array}$$ Use 10.

$$\begin{array}{r} 10 \\ -\ 2 \\ \hline 8 \end{array}$$ Use counters.

Sometimes one way is easier than another.

Subtract. Tell how you found each difference.

1.
$$\begin{array}{r} 12 \\ -\ 11 \end{array} \qquad \begin{array}{r} 10 \\ -\ 7 \end{array} \qquad \begin{array}{r} 17 \\ -\ 9 \end{array} \qquad \begin{array}{r} 14 \\ -\ 6 \end{array} \qquad \begin{array}{r} 7 \\ -\ 3 \end{array} \qquad \begin{array}{r} 13 \\ -\ 11 \end{array}$$

2.
$$\begin{array}{r} 18 \\ -\ 9 \end{array} \qquad \begin{array}{r} 8 \\ -\ 2 \end{array} \qquad \begin{array}{r} 13 \\ -\ 5 \end{array} \qquad \begin{array}{r} 14 \\ -\ 5 \end{array} \qquad \begin{array}{r} 16 \\ -\ 7 \end{array} \qquad \begin{array}{r} 12 \\ -\ 7 \end{array}$$

3.
$$\begin{array}{r} 16 \\ -\ 9 \end{array} \qquad \begin{array}{r} 15 \\ -\ 6 \end{array} \qquad \begin{array}{r} 12 \\ -\ 6 \end{array} \qquad \begin{array}{r} 10 \\ -\ 4 \end{array} \qquad \begin{array}{r} 14 \\ -\ 9 \end{array} \qquad \begin{array}{r} 9 \\ -\ 0 \end{array}$$

Home Connection Write 2 or 3 problems similar to the ones on this page. Ask your child to solve the problems and describe the strategy he or she used to find each answer.

three hundred thirty-one   **331**

Follow the path to add and subtract.
Write the missing numbers.

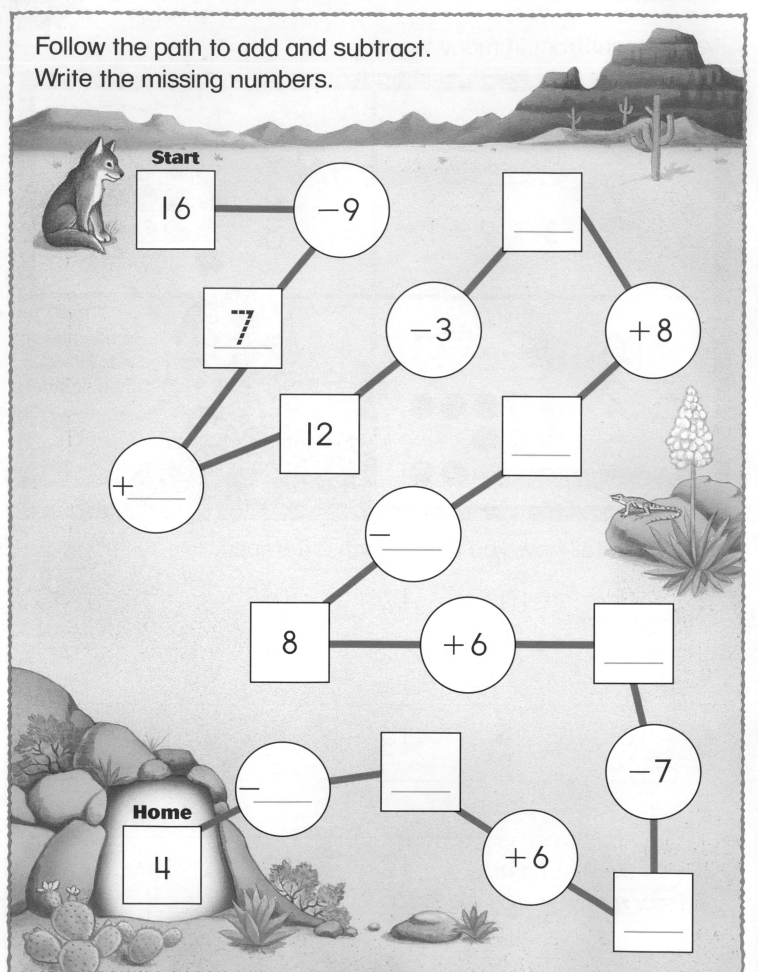

Start

16 → −9 → [___] → +8

7 → −3 → [___]

+___ → 12 → [− ___]

8 → +6 → [___]

[− ___] → [___] → +6 → −7 → [___]

Home

4

© Silver Burdett Ginn Inc. All rights reserved.

Name_____

Read carefully.

Think: What do I need to find out?

Cross out the information you do not need.

Write the number sentence.

1. Nancy sees 7 white flowers.
   ~~She sees 6 green lizards.~~
   She sees 8 pink flowers.
   How many flowers does she see?

   $\underline{7} \oplus \underline{8} = \underline{15}$ flowers

---

2. Kurt counts 17 butterflies.
   Then 9 butterflies fly away.
   6 beetles crawl away.
   How many butterflies are there now?

   _____ ◯ _____ = _____ butterflies

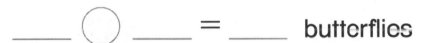

---

3. Jenny sees 8 big deer and 6 little deer.
   The deer are behind
   How many deer does she see altogether?

   _____ ◯ _____ = _____ deer

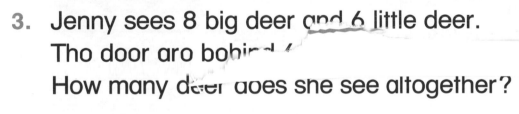
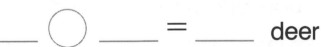

---

4. Alex sees 18 lizards.
   The lizards are on 2 rocks.
   9 of the lizards hide.
   How many lizards are left?

   _____ ◯ _____ = _____ lizards

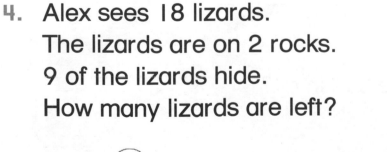

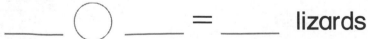
Home Connection Make up word problems with extra information for your child to solve. Ask what is extra.

Cross out the information you do not need.
Write the number sentence.

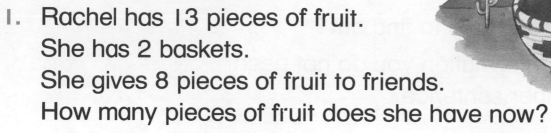

1. Rachel has 13 pieces of fruit.
   She has 2 baskets.
   She gives 8 pieces of fruit to friends.
   How many pieces of fruit does she have now?

   _____ ◯ _____ = _____ pieces of fruit

2. Cody's family sees 16 deer.
   8 deer run away.
   Cody sees 2 bobcats.
   How many deer are left?

   _____ ◯ _____ = _____ deer

3. José sees 4 owls.
   He sees 6 bats.
   He sees 8 deer.
   How many bats and owls does José see?

   _____ ◯ _____ = _____ bats and owls

4. Sara sees 7 birds.
   Then she sees 4 more.
   Sara sees 8 squirrels.
   How many birds does she see in all?

   _____ ◯ _____ = _____ birds

Add.

1.

6	7	4	9	8	7
4	5	4	2	2	3
+ 2	+ 5	+ 5	+ 2	+ 1	+ 2

Subtract.

2. $14 - 9 =$ ___ $13 - 8 =$ ___ $16 - 7 =$ ___

3. $15 - 7 =$ ___ $17 - 8 =$ ___ $14 - 6 =$ ___

Add or subtract.

4.  $4 + 9 =$ ___ $13 - 9 =$ ___

$9 + 4 =$ ___ $13 - 4 =$ ___

5.  $9 + 6 =$ ___ $15 - 6 =$ ___

$6 + 9 =$ ___ $15 - 9 =$ ___

Cross out the information you do not need.
Write a number sentence.

6. Toby sees 5 deer.
She sees 14 cactuses.
She sees 9 more deer.
How many deer does Toby see?

___ ◯ ___ = ___ deer

Where is the largest desert in the world?

Add or subtract to find out.
Color each sum or difference.

less than 9 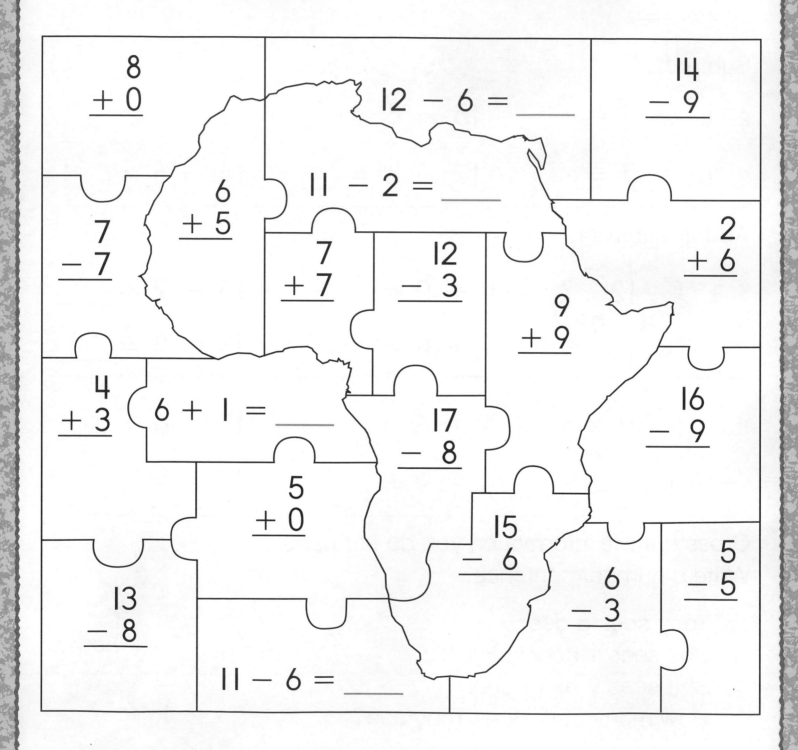 blue

9 or greater green

8
+ 0

12 − 6 = ____

14
− 9

7
− 7

6
+ 5

11 − 2 = ____

2
+ 6

7
+ 7

12
− 3

9
+ 9

4
+ 3

6 + 1 = ____

17
− 8

16
− 9

5
+ 0

15
− 6

5
− 5

6
− 3

13
− 8

11 − 6 = ____

Name_____

Add or subtract.

1.

$$\begin{array}{r} 9 \\ + 5 \\ \hline \end{array} \quad \begin{array}{r} 8 \\ + 8 \\ \hline \end{array} \quad \begin{array}{r} 9 \\ + 9 \\ \hline \end{array} \quad \begin{array}{r} 8 \\ + 9 \\ \hline \end{array} \quad \begin{array}{r} 4 \\ 1 \\ + 9 \\ \hline \end{array} \quad \begin{array}{r} 5 \\ 5 \\ + 3 \\ \hline \end{array}$$

2.

$$\begin{array}{r} 10 \\ - 5 \\ \hline \end{array} \quad \begin{array}{r} 12 \\ - 7 \\ \hline \end{array} \quad \begin{array}{r} 13 \\ - 9 \\ \hline \end{array} \quad \begin{array}{r} 17 \\ - 8 \\ \hline \end{array} \quad \begin{array}{r} 11 \\ - 9 \\ \hline \end{array} \quad \begin{array}{r} 12 \\ - 6 \\ \hline \end{array}$$

3. $15 - 7 = $ _____ $12 - 8 = $ _____ $17 - 9 = $ _____

Add or subtract.

4.  $8 + 7 = $ ___ $15 - 7 = $ ___

   $7 + 8 = $ ___ $15 - 8 = $ ___

5.  $9 + 3 = $ ___ $12 - 3 = $ ___

   $3 + 9 = $ ___ $12 - 9 = $ ___

Write a number sentence.

6. 3 hawks rest in a tree.
   9 hawks join them.
   How many are there now? ____ ____ = ____ hawks

7. 12 foxes drink at a stream.
   8 run away.
   How many are there now? ____ ____ = ____ foxes

Name_____ **Performance Assessment**

What You Need

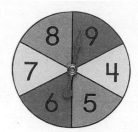

spinner

---

① Spin the spinner 2 times.
   Record each number.

② Use the numbers to write an addition sentence.
   Then write a related subtraction sentence.

	Spin 1	**Spin 2**	**Number Sentences**
1.			____ + ____ = ____ ____ − ____ = ____
2.			____ + ____ = ____ ____ − ____ = ____
3.			____ + ____ = ____ ____ − ____ = ____

4. Look at the sentences you wrote.
   Tell other related number sentences.

For Your Portfolio
You might put this page in your portfolio.

Name_____

Complete each table.
Look for a pattern.

1.

foxes	1	2	3	4	5	6
legs	4	8	12			

2.

rabbits	1	2	3	4	5	6
ears	2	4				

3.

cactuses	1	2	3	4	5	6
flowers	3	6				

4.

feet	1	2	3	4	5	6
toes	5	10				

Journal Idea

 Make your own table.
How can you check your answers?

Name_____

Use a .

Circle + or − .

Remember to press ON/C before you begin each exercise.

1. **8** **7** **9** = 10

2. **6** + − **5** + − **7** = 18

3. **1** + − **8** + − **3** = 6

4. **9** + − **4** + − **8** = 13

5. **7** + − **6** + − **7** = 8

6. **4** + − **9** + − **2** = 11

7. **5** + − **9** + − **5** = 9

8. **9** + − **3** + − **8** = 14

340   three hundred forty

Cumulative Review
Preparing for Tests

Name_____

Fill in the ⬭ for the correct answer.

Add or subtract.

1.
$$3 + 2$$
- ⬭ 8
- ⬭ 6
- ⬭ 1
- ⬭ 5

2.
$$8 - 7$$
- ⬭ 0
- ⬭ 1
- ⬭ 2
- ⬭ 3

3.
$$11 - 5$$
- ⬭ 1
- ⬭ 6
- ⬭ 7
- ⬭ 8

4.
$$12¢ - 4¢$$
- ⬭ 8¢
- ⬭ 10¢
- ⬭ 4¢
- ⬭ 7¢

5.
$$9 + 9$$
- ⬭ 0
- ⬭ 15
- ⬭ 18
- ⬭ 16

6.
$$8 + 5$$
- ⬭ 13
- ⬭ 12
- ⬭ 15
- ⬭ 14

7.
$$16 - 9$$
- ⬭ 9
- ⬭ 8
- ⬭ 7
- ⬭ 6

8.
$$3 + 7 + 2$$
- ⬭ 10
- ⬭ 15
- ⬭ 16
- ⬭ 12

9.
$$4 + 8 + 4$$
- ⬭ 12
- ⬭ 16
- ⬭ 15
- ⬭ 17

10. How much money is there?

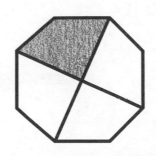

- ⬭ 32¢
- ⬭ 30¢
- ⬭ 41¢
- ⬭ 46¢

11. How many equal parts are there?

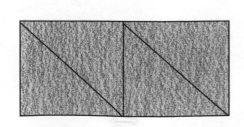

- ⬭ 1
- ⬭ 5
- ⬭ 2
- ⬭ 4

12. What part is red?

- ⬭ $\frac{1}{2}$
- ⬭ $\frac{1}{3}$
- ⬭ $\frac{1}{4}$

What time is it?

13.
- ◯ 4:00
- ⬤ 3:00
- ◯ 3:30
- ◯ 12:00

14.
- ◯ 6:30
- ◯ 4:30
- ⬤ 5:30
- ◯ 7:30

15.
- ◯ 6:00
- ◯ 6:30
- ◯ 10:00
- ⬤ 9:30

16.
- ⬤ 12:30
- ◯ 6:00
- ◯ 12:00
- ◯ 6:30

17. Does this hold **more** or **less** than 1 liter?
- ⬤ more
- ◯ less

18. About how long is this real object?
- ◯ about 1 inch
- ◯ about 4 inches
- ⬤ about 12 inches

Which tool would you use to measure?

19. How long is it?

⬤ ◯ ◯

20. How heavy is it?

◯ ◯ ⬤

Chapter 11 Cumulative Review

© Silver Burdett Ginn Inc. All rights reserved.

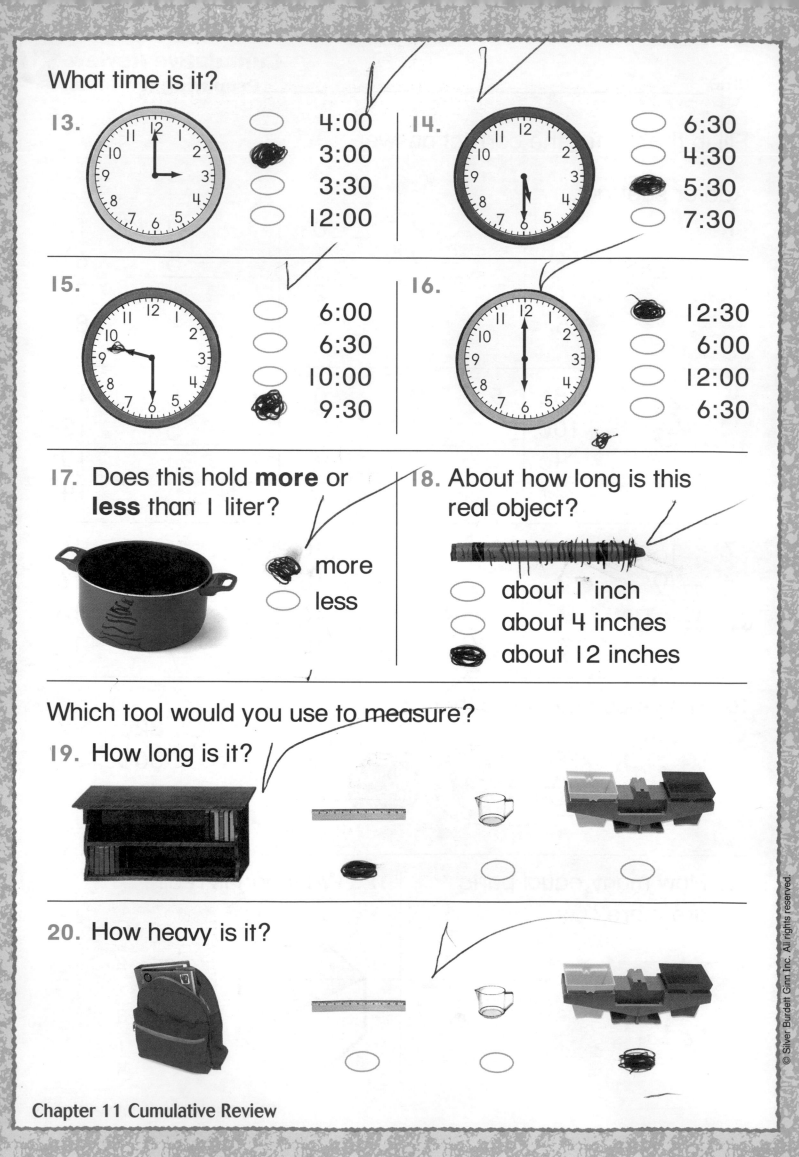

Exploring Two-Digit Addition and Subtraction

Po Lan's Pocket

written by Jerry Melvin

illustrated by Judy Moffatt

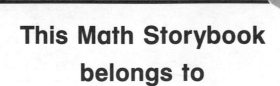

This Math Storybook

belongs to

_____

Po Lan has a pocket.
It's a very special kind.
It can fit most anything
that she seems to find.

© Silver Burdett Ginn Inc. All rights reserved.

B

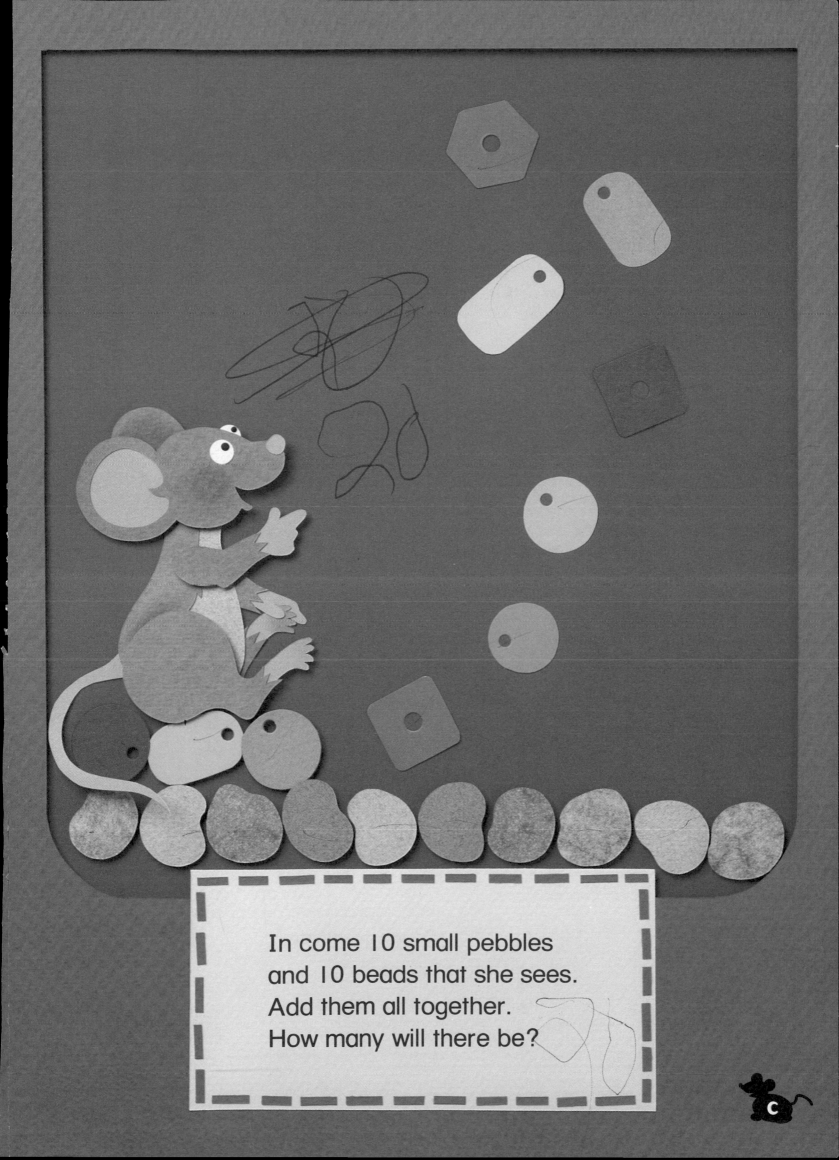

In come 10 small pebbles
and 10 beads that she sees.
Add them all together.
How many will there be?

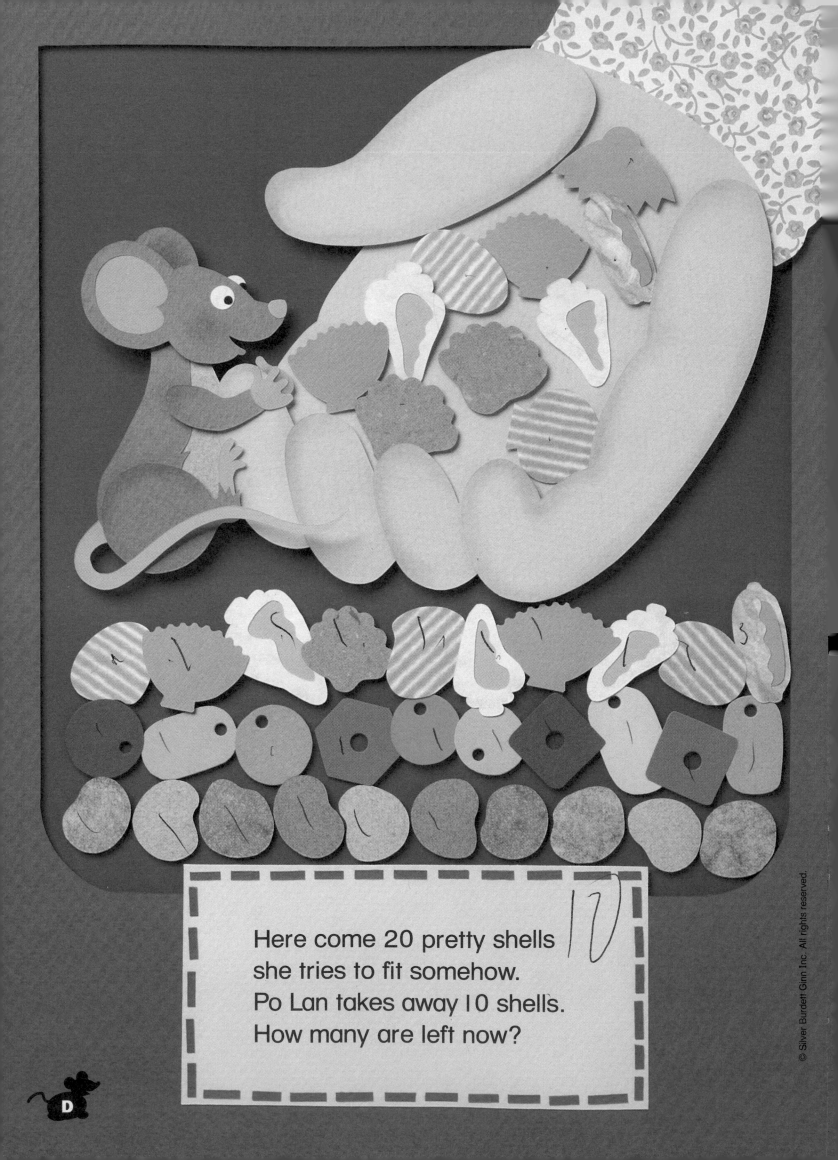

Here come 20 pretty shells
she tries to fit somehow.
Po Lan takes away 10 shells.
How many are left now?

© Silver Burdett Ginn Inc. All rights reserved.

Here come 10 brown acorns.
She drops them and they fall.
She drops 10 seeds on top of them.
How many things are there in all?

Here come 2 new jacks.
And 3 leaves from a tree.
But the best thing Po Lan finds
is something just for me!

© Silver Burdett Ginn Inc. All rights reserved.

Draw some things that you like.
Then count up what you see.
If you had 10 more of them,
how many would there be?

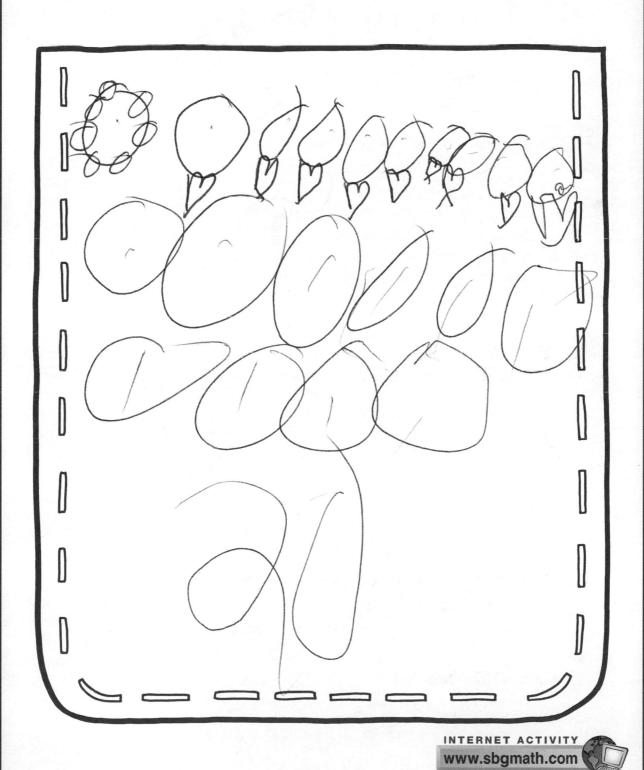

G

A Note to the Family

Here are some learning ideas you can share with your child.

Enjoy *Po Lan's Pocket* Together

- Read the story with your child. Ask your child to find the total number of items in Po Lan's pocket. Then talk about how to find how many there are if more are added or if some are taken away.

- Encourage your child to show you what he or she drew in the pocket on the last page of the story. Ask your child to make up addition and subtraction stories about things that might be found in their pockets.

At-Home Activity

- Show your child a group of common household items such as pasta, buttons, pennies, paper clips, or dry cereal. Add some to the group and ask your child to tell how many there are in all. Repeat the activity, removing some from the group and asking your child to find how many are left.

Read More About It!

To read more stories about addition and subtraction with your child, look for these books in your local library.

- *Hold Tight, Bear!* by Ron Maris (Harcourt Brace, 1993)

- *Sea Sums* by Joy N. Hulme (Hyperion Books for Children, 1996)

- *Yellow Ball* by Molly Bang (Puffin Books, 1993)

Visit Our Web Site!

INTERNET ACTIVITY
www.sbgmath.com

© Silver Burdett Ginn Inc. All rights reserved.

H

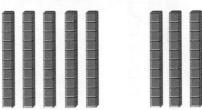

Adding tens is like adding ones.

5 ones + 3 ones   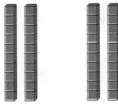 5 tens + 3 tens

5 + 3 = 8   50 + 30 = 80

Write the numbers. Add.

Use models and Workmat 5 if you like.

1.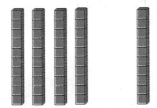

____ tens + ____ ten

____ + ____ = ____

2.

____ tens + ____ tens

____ + ____ = ____

3.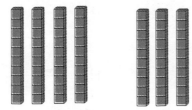

____ tens + ____ tens

____ + ____ = ____

4.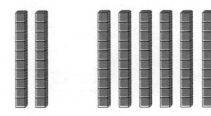

____ tens + ____ tens

____ + ____ = ____

Write the numbers. Add.
Use models if you like.

1.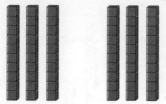

   _3_ tens + _3_ tens

   30 + 30 = 60

2.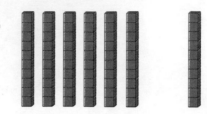

   ___ tens + ___ ten

   ___ + ___ = ___

3.

   ___ tens + ___ tens

   ___ + ___ = ___

4.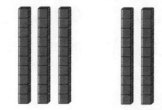

   ___ tens + ___ tens

   ___ + ___ = ___

 Critical Thinking Corner   Using Algebra

Number Sense   Journal Idea

Find each sum. Look for a pattern.

4 tens + 4 tens = ___ tens   40 + 40 = ___

5 tens + 5 tens = ___ tens   50 + 50 = ___

6 tens + 6 tens = ___ tens   60 + 60 = ___

 What comes next in the pattern? Tell how you know.

© Silver Burdett Ginn Inc. All rights reserved.

You can count on to add.

Start with 32.
Count on 3 ones.
32, 33, 34, 35

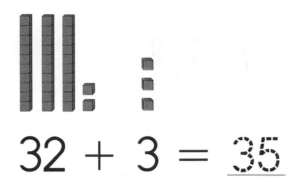

32 + 3 = 35

Use models and Workmat 5.
Count on to add.
Write how many in all.

	Number	Add	Number in all
1.	16	2	18
2.	42	3	
3.	30	3	
4.	55	1	
5.	22	2	
6.	61	3	
7.	27	2	
8.	36	3	

Home Connection Counting on 1, 2, or 3 can help your child learn to add. Choose a two-digit number. Then ask your child to add 1, 2, or 3 to that number.

three hundred forty-three **343**

Write each number.
Circle the greater number.
Count on to add.

1.

$$\left(\widehat{21}\right) + \underline{3} = \underline{24}$$

2.

$$\underline{} + \underline{} = \underline{}$$

3.

$$\underline{} + \underline{} = \underline{}$$

4.

$$\underline{} + \underline{} = \underline{}$$

 Problem Solving

Count on with pennies.
How much money will there be
in each pocket?

5.

24¢

_____ ¢

6.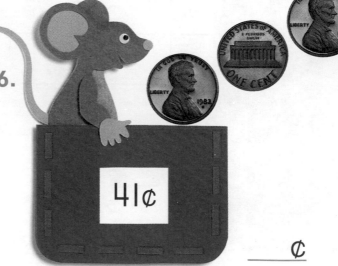

41¢

_____ ¢

© Silver Burdett Ginn Inc. All rights reserved.

Name_____

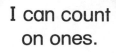 I can count
on ones.
24, 25, 26, 27

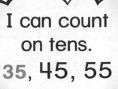 I can count
on tens.
35, 45, 55

24 + 3 = 27

35 + 20 = 55

Add. Count on ones or tens.

1.
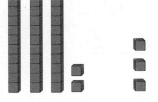

32 + 3 = ___

2.
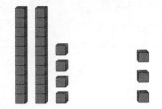

26 + 30 = ___

3.
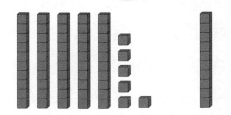

56 + 10 = ___

4.
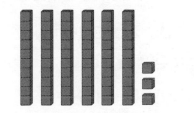

63 + 2 = ___

Home Connection Your child is learning to add ones or tens
to a two-digit number. Ask your child to tell you whether he or she
counted on by ones or tens for each exercise on this page.

Add. Count on ones or tens.
Start with the greater number.
Use models if you like.

1. $\begin{array}{r} 36 \\ +\ 2 \\ \hline 38 \end{array}$ 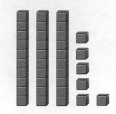 $\begin{array}{r} 25 \\ +30 \\ \hline \end{array}$

2. $\begin{array}{r} 43 \\ +\ 2 \\ \hline \end{array}$ $\begin{array}{r} 51 \\ +20 \\ \hline \end{array}$ $\begin{array}{r} 38 \\ +10 \\ \hline \end{array}$ $\begin{array}{r} 10 \\ +\ 3 \\ \hline \end{array}$ $\begin{array}{r} 69 \\ +10 \\ \hline \end{array}$ $\begin{array}{r} 30 \\ +30 \\ \hline \end{array}$

3. $\begin{array}{r} 35 \\ +\ 3 \\ \hline \end{array}$ $\begin{array}{r} 66 \\ +\ 1 \\ \hline \end{array}$ $\begin{array}{r} 26 \\ +20 \\ \hline \end{array}$ $\begin{array}{r} 32 \\ +\ 3 \\ \hline \end{array}$ $\begin{array}{r} 11 \\ +\ 2 \\ \hline \end{array}$ $\begin{array}{r} 53 \\ +\ 2 \\ \hline \end{array}$

4. $\begin{array}{r} 42 \\ +20 \\ \hline \end{array}$ $\begin{array}{r} 17 \\ +\ 2 \\ \hline \end{array}$ $\begin{array}{r} 80 \\ +\ 1 \\ \hline \end{array}$ $\begin{array}{r} 76 \\ +\ 2 \\ \hline \end{array}$ $\begin{array}{r} 64 \\ +\ 2 \\ \hline \end{array}$ $\begin{array}{r} 10 \\ +78 \\ \hline \end{array}$

Problem Solving

Solve.

5. Randy has 15 shells.
    He finds 2 more.
    How many shells
    does he have now?

    _____ shells

6. What if Randy finds
    20 more shells?
    Now how many shells
    will he have?

    _____ shells

© Silver Burdett Ginn Inc. All rights reserved.

Name_____ **Adding Two-Digit Numbers**

How many seeds are there in all?

32

---

1 First add the ones.

Tens	Ones
3	2
+ 1	1
	3

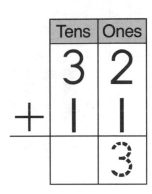

2 Then add the tens.

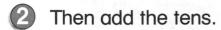

Tens	Ones
3	2
+ 1	1
4	3

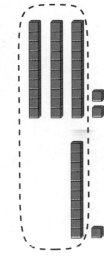

Use models and Workmat 5.
Find each sum.

1.

Tens	Ones
3	5
+ 4	2
7	7

Tens	Ones
5	1
+ 2	3

Tens	Ones
4	3
+	6

Tens	Ones
2	2
+ 6	0

2.

Tens	Ones
3	4
+ 2	2

Tens	Ones
4	9
+ 2	0

Tens	Ones
3	6
+	2

Tens	Ones
2	7
+ 7	2

Home Connection Your child is learning to add two-digit numbers. Ask your child to tell how she or he found each sum on this page.

three hundred forty-seven **347**

Find each sum.

1.

Tens	Ones
2	4
+ 3	0
5	4

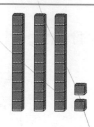

2.

Tens	Ones
4	6
+ 5	2
4	8

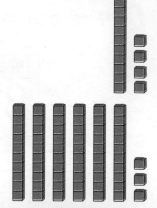

3.

Tens	Ones
3	2
+	5

4.

Tens	Ones
1	4
+ 6	3

© Silver Burdett Ginn Inc. All rights reserved.

✓ Checkpoint

Add. Count on ones or tens.

1.

56 + 10 = ____

2.

31 + 3 = ____

3.

25	48	72	69	55	33
+20	+10	+ 3	+20	+ 2	+30

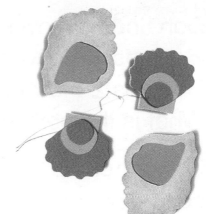

On Monday, James picks up 4 shells.
On Tuesday he picks up 8 shells.
On Wednesday he picks up 12 shells.
If James continues the pattern, how
many shells will he pick up on Friday?

 Understand

You need to find out how many shells
James will pick up on Friday.

 Plan

Look for the pattern. Then continue it.

> 4 + 4 = 8 and
> 8 + 4 = 12

 Solve

The pattern is to add __4__ more shells each day.

Monday	Tuesday	Wednesday	Thursday	Friday
4	8	12	16	20

James will pick up __20__ shells on Friday.

 Look Back

Did you answer the question?

Find a pattern.

1. Eva collects 5 baseball cards in March.
   She collects 10 cards in April. She collects
   15 cards in May. What is the pattern?

   The pattern is to add _____ more cards each month.

Home Connection Ask your child to tell you about
each pattern on this page then tell what would come next.

Find the pattern. Solve.

1. Dan finds 8 leaves in 1 hour.
   He finds 16 leaves after 2 hours.
   He finds 24 leaves after 3 hours.
   What is the pattern?

   The pattern is to add _____ more leaves
   each hour.

2. What if Dan continues this pattern?
   How many leaves will he find after 5 hours?

1 hour	2 hours	3 hours	4 hours	5 hours
8	16	24		

   Dan will find _____ leaves after 5 hours.

3. Tina is making a banner with green
   and blue triangles.
   She puts the triangles in this pattern.

   What is the pattern? _____

   _____

4. Color to continue Tina's pattern.
   How many blue and green triangles
   will she need in all?

© Silver Burdett Ginn Inc. All rights reserved.

There are many ways to add.

You can count on ones.
32, 33, 34, 35

You can count on tens.
29, 39, 49, 59

You can use models.

$$\begin{array}{r} 32 \\ +\ 3 \\ \hline 35 \end{array}$$

$$\begin{array}{r} 29 \\ +30 \\ \hline 59 \end{array}$$

$$\begin{array}{r} 21 \\ +15 \\ \hline 36 \end{array}$$

Can you think of other ways?

Add. Tell how you found each sum.
Use models when you like.

1.
$$\begin{array}{r} 17 \\ +70 \end{array}$$
$$\begin{array}{r} 23 \\ +61 \end{array}$$
$$\begin{array}{r} 31 \\ +\ 5 \end{array}$$
$$\begin{array}{r} 72 \\ +14 \end{array}$$
$$\begin{array}{r} 26 \\ +50 \end{array}$$
$$\begin{array}{r} 43 \\ +34 \end{array}$$

2.
$$\begin{array}{r} 62 \\ +\ 6 \end{array}$$
$$\begin{array}{r} 30 \\ +26 \end{array}$$
$$\begin{array}{r} 41 \\ +24 \end{array}$$
$$\begin{array}{r} 81 \\ +\ 2 \end{array}$$
$$\begin{array}{r} 49 \\ +40 \end{array}$$
$$\begin{array}{r} 26 \\ +62 \end{array}$$

3.
$$\begin{array}{r} 13 \\ +62 \end{array}$$
$$\begin{array}{r} 86 \\ +10 \end{array}$$
$$\begin{array}{r} 44 \\ +13 \end{array}$$
$$\begin{array}{r} 37 \\ +11 \end{array}$$
$$\begin{array}{r} 21 \\ +\ 7 \end{array}$$
$$\begin{array}{r} 52 \\ +22 \end{array}$$

Home Connection Ask your child how he or she solved some of the exercises on this page. Discuss the different strategies and when one is better than another.

three hundred fifty-one **351**

Conner made a table to show his card collection.

Trading Cards

Type of Card	Number
Football	23
Hockey	21
Baseball	61
Soccer	16

Use the table to solve.
Tell how you found each sum.

1. How many football and hockey cards does Conner have?

   __44__ cards

   $$\begin{array}{r} 23 \\ + 21 \\ \hline 44 \end{array}$$

2. Jackie has 31 soccer cards.
   How many do Conner and Jackie have together?

   ____ cards

   $$\begin{array}{r} \\ + \\ \hline \end{array}$$

3. Conner gets 30 more hockey cards.
   How many does he have now?

   ____ cards

   $$\begin{array}{r} \\ + \\ \hline \end{array}$$

4. Conner finds 2 baseball cards.
   How many does he have now?

   ____ cards

   $$\begin{array}{r} \\ + \\ \hline \end{array}$$

© Silver Burdett Ginn Inc. All rights reserved.

Subtracting tens is like subtracting ones.

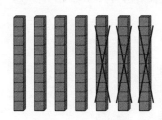

_7_ ones — _3_ ones   _7_ tens — _3_ tens

_7_ — _3_ = _4_   _70_ — _30_ = _40_

Write the numbers. Subtract.
Use models if you like.

1.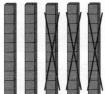

____ tens — ____ ten

____ — ____ = ____

2.

____ tens — ____ tens

____ — ____ = ____

3.

____ tens — ____ tens

____ — ____ = ____

4.

____ tens — ____ tens

____ — ____ = ____

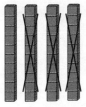

Home Connection Your child is learning to use basic facts to help him or her subtract tens. Ask your child to subtract numbers that are multiples of ten.

Write the numbers. Subtract.
Use models if you like.

1.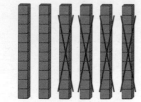

___6___ tens – ___4___ tens

_60_ – _40_ = _20_

2.

_____ tens – _____ tens

___ – ___ = ___

3.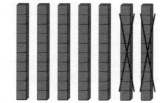

_____ tens – _____ tens

___ – ___ = ___

4.

_____ tens – _____ ten

___ – ___ = ___

 Critical Thinking Corner Using Algebra

Number Sense   Journal Idea

 Look for a pattern. Subtract. Tell how you found each difference.

$8 - 4 = $ _____

$80 - 40 = $ _____

$800 - 400 = $ _____

© Silver Burdett Ginn Inc. All rights reserved.

Name_____

You can count back
to subtract ones.

Start at 38.
Count back 3 ones.
38, 37, 36, 35

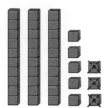

$$38 - 3 = 35$$

Use models and Workmat 5.
Count back to subtract.
Write how many are left.

	Number	Subtract	Difference
1.	48	2	46
2.	66	1	
3.	49	2	
4.	17	3	
5.	25	1	
6.	38	3	
7.	74	2	
8.	57	1	

Home Connection Your child is learning to subtract
1, 2, or 3 from a two-digit number by counting back. Choose
a number like 27 or 39. Ask your child to subtract 1, 2, or 3.

Count back to subtract.

1.

$25 - 3 = \underline{22}$

2.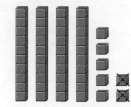

$47 - 2 = \underline{}$

3.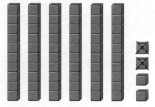

$64 - 2 = \underline{}$

4.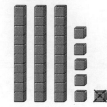

$36 - 1 = \underline{}$

5.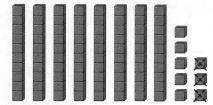

$88 - 3 = \underline{}$

6.

$74 - 3 = \underline{}$

PROBLEM SOLVING

Problem Solving

Using Algebra

Find each rule.
Use models if you like.

7. Subtract _2_

59	57
46	44
37	35

8. Subtract ____

34	33
89	88
76	75

9. Subtract ____

77	74
26	23
49	46

© Silver Burdett Ginn Inc. All rights reserved.

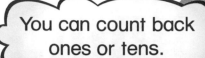
You can count back ones or tens.

45, 44, 43

$$45 - 2 = 43$$

32, 22, 12

$$32 - 20 = 12$$

Count back ones or tens to subtract.

1.
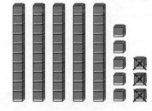

$$58 - 3 = \underline{\hspace{1cm}}$$

2.
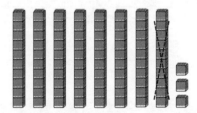

$$83 - 10 = \underline{\hspace{1cm}}$$

3.

$$44 - 30 = \underline{\hspace{1cm}}$$

4.
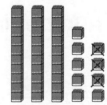

$$39 - 3 = \underline{\hspace{1cm}}$$

Home Connection Your child is counting back tens or ones to subtract. Ask your child to tell you how he or she counted back in each exercise on this page.

three hundred fifty-seven **357**

Subtract. Count back ones or tens.
Use models if you like.

1. $\begin{array}{r} 47 \\ -\ 2 \\ \hline 45 \end{array}$ 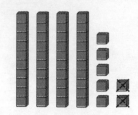 $\begin{array}{r} 88 \\ -20 \\ \hline \end{array}$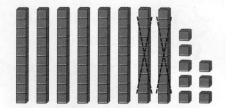

2. $\begin{array}{r} 43 \\ -\ 2 \\ \hline \end{array}$ $\begin{array}{r} 51 \\ -20 \\ \hline \end{array}$ $\begin{array}{r} 98 \\ -10 \\ \hline \end{array}$ $\begin{array}{r} 13 \\ -\ 3 \\ \hline \end{array}$ $\begin{array}{r} 69 \\ -30 \\ \hline \end{array}$ $\begin{array}{r} 20 \\ -20 \\ \hline \end{array}$

3. $\begin{array}{r} 36 \\ -\ 1 \\ \hline \end{array}$ $\begin{array}{r} 66 \\ -\ 3 \\ \hline \end{array}$ $\begin{array}{r} 76 \\ -30 \\ \hline \end{array}$ $\begin{array}{r} 55 \\ -\ 2 \\ \hline \end{array}$ $\begin{array}{r} 24 \\ -10 \\ \hline \end{array}$ $\begin{array}{r} 37 \\ -\ 3 \\ \hline \end{array}$

4. $\begin{array}{r} 28 \\ -\ 3 \\ \hline \end{array}$ $\begin{array}{r} 85 \\ -20 \\ \hline \end{array}$ $\begin{array}{r} 45 \\ -\ 1 \\ \hline \end{array}$ $\begin{array}{r} 16 \\ -10 \\ \hline \end{array}$ $\begin{array}{r} 36 \\ -20 \\ \hline \end{array}$ $\begin{array}{r} 29 \\ -\ 2 \\ \hline \end{array}$

 Critical Thinking Corner — Using Algebra

Mental Math

Do you subtract 2 or 20?
Write the correct number in each shape.

5. $62 - \triangle = 42$

6. $78 - \square = 76$

7. $45 - \bigcirc = 43$

8. $95 - \hexagon = 75$

© Silver Burdett Ginn Inc. All rights reserved.

How many more shells does Rosie have?

1 First subtract the ones.

Tens	Ones
5	9
− 2	4
	5

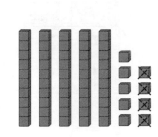

2 Then subtract the tens.

Tens	Ones
5	9
− 2	4
3	5

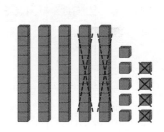

Use models and Workmat 5.
Find each difference.

1.

Tens	Ones
6	9
− 3	5
3	4

Tens	Ones
5	8
− 2	1

Tens	Ones
9	6
− 3	2

Tens	Ones
7	5
− 5	3

2.

Tens	Ones
3	4
− 2	0

Tens	Ones
4	9
− 2	4

Tens	Ones
6	7
−	4

Tens	Ones
3	9
− 1	2

Cross out to subtract.

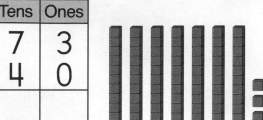

Remember, subtract the ones first.

1.

Tens	Ones
6	5
− 2	3
4	2

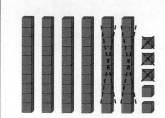

2.

Tens	Ones
7	3
− 4	0

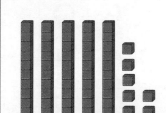

3.

Tens	Ones
5	9
−	4

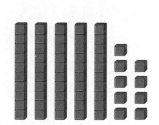

4.

Tens	Ones
5	7
− 1	2

5.

Tens	Ones
4	8
− 2	3

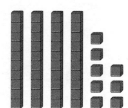

6.

Tens	Ones
3	7
−	2

Problem Solving

Solve.

7. Ben has 27 feathers.
He finds 10 more.
Then he loses 3.
How many feathers does he have now? _____ feathers

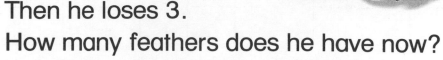

© Silver Burdett Ginn Inc. All rights reserved.

There are many ways to subtract.

You can count back ones.
47, 46, 45, 44

You can count back tens.
58, 48, 38

You can use models.

```
  47
-  3
  44
```

```
  58
- 20
  38
```

```
  36
- 12
  24
```

How do you like to subtract?
Can you think of another way?

Subtract.
Tell how you found each difference.
Use models when you like.

1.
```
  89        73        66        38        67        56
- 71       -50       - 3       -12       -23       - 2
```

2.
```
  77        28        91        58        38        64
- 31       - 7       -40       - 1       -24       -30
```

3.
```
  43        65        76        64        75        29
- 10       - 2       -51       -42       -34       - 2
```

Home Connection Ask your child to tell you how he or she found each difference on this page. Discuss when to use each strategy.

three hundred sixty-one   **361**

Add or subtract.
Tell how you found
each sum or difference.

1. 90   56   71   30   66   43
   −30   −32   −11   −30   −33   −31
    60

2. 67   34   52   38   64   89
   − 6   −22   −41   −10   −12   −66

3. 67   41   28   53   74   21
   + 2   +30   +10   + 3   + 2   +30

4. 60 − 20 = _____   75 − 2 = _____

5. 20 + 40 = _____   50 + 3 = _____

What Do You Think?

Journal Idea

I think sometimes one way to
subtract is better than another.
What do you think?

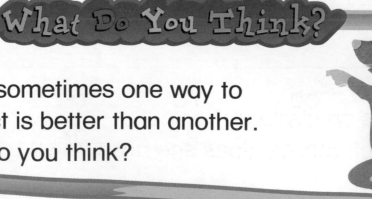

© Silver Burdett Ginn Inc. All rights reserved.

Name_____

APPLICATION

Understand

Plan

Look Back

Solve

Problem Solving
Using Money

Use the picture to solve.

Think: Do you need to add or subtract?

1. Jesse has 56¢.
   He buys a bag of marbles.
   How much money does he have now?

   $$\begin{array}{r} 56¢ \\ -\ 35¢ \\ \hline 21¢ \end{array}$$

2. Alice buys a trading card.
   Then she buys a book.
   How much money did she spend?

   _____ ¢
          ¢
          ¢

3. Paco buys a box of shells.
   He also buys a car.
   How much money did he spend?

   _____ ¢
          ¢
          ¢

4. Beth has 98¢.
   She buys an airplane.
   How much money does she have now?

   _____ ¢
          ¢
          ¢

Home Connection Put price tags up to 50¢ on several toys.
"Go shopping" with your child to practice adding and subtracting.

Use the picture. Add or subtract to solve.

1. Luis has 69¢.
He buys a pencil.
How much money does he have now?

_____ ¢
¢
¢

2. Molly buys a notebook.
She also buys a ruler.
How much does she spend?

_____ ¢
¢
¢

3. Tal has 77¢.
He buys a pad.
How much money does he have now?

_____ ¢
¢
¢

4. Choose 2 things to buy. Then solve.

Make Your Own

I buy a _____ .

Then I buy a _____ .

How much do I spend?

_____ ¢
¢
¢

© Silver Burdett Ginn Inc. All rights reserved.

Subtract. Count back ones or tens.

1.
37	58	74	59	45	63
− 2	−10	− 1	−20	− 3	−30
35		73		42	

2.
75	18	32	66	36	39
−30	− 2	−10	−20	− 1	− 3
	16				36

Cross out to subtract.

3.

Tens	Ones
6	4
− 2	1

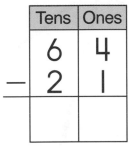

4.

Tens	Ones
4	7
− 2	0

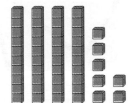

Use the pictures to solve.

5. Sal buys 2 shells.
   How much does he spend?

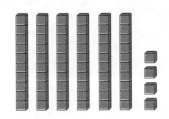

¢
_____ ¢
¢

shells
12¢ each

6. Lynne has 66¢.
   She buys a rock.
   How much does she
   have now?

¢
_____ ¢
¢

rocks
23¢ each

three hundred sixty-five   **365**

Name_____

Add or subtract.

Color each sum or difference. greater than 50 ((blue))

less than 50 ((red))

equal to 50 ((yellow))

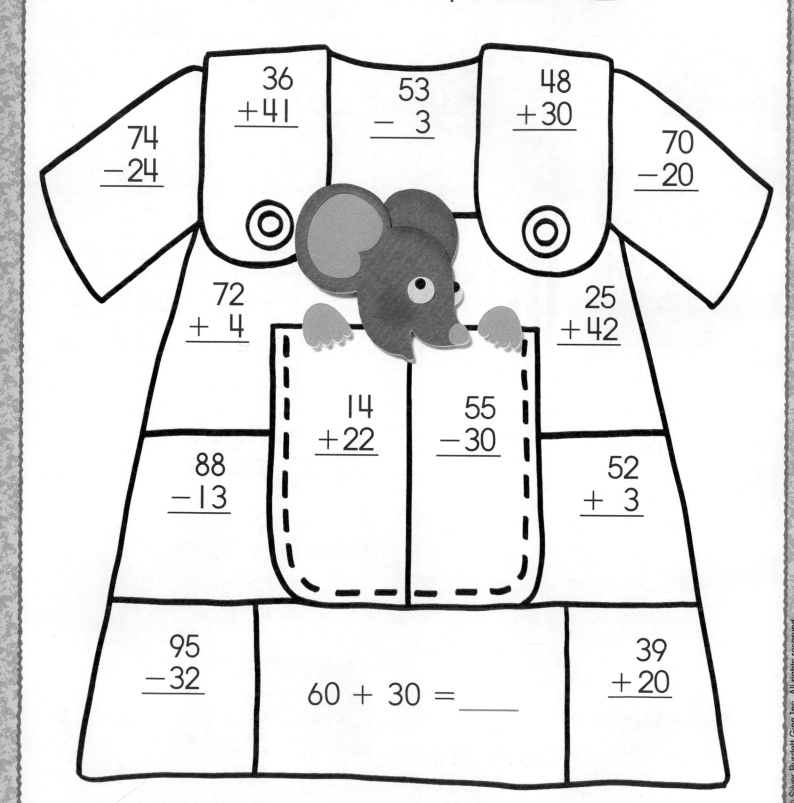

$$\begin{array}{r} 74 \\ -24 \\ \hline \end{array}$$

$$\begin{array}{r} 36 \\ +41 \\ \hline \end{array}$$

$$\begin{array}{r} 53 \\ -3 \\ \hline \end{array}$$

$$\begin{array}{r} 48 \\ +30 \\ \hline \end{array}$$

$$\begin{array}{r} 70 \\ -20 \\ \hline \end{array}$$

$$\begin{array}{r} 72 \\ +4 \\ \hline \end{array}$$

$$\begin{array}{r} 25 \\ +42 \\ \hline \end{array}$$

$$\begin{array}{r} 14 \\ +22 \\ \hline \end{array}$$

$$\begin{array}{r} 55 \\ -30 \\ \hline \end{array}$$

$$\begin{array}{r} 88 \\ -13 \\ \hline \end{array}$$

$$\begin{array}{r} 52 \\ +3 \\ \hline \end{array}$$

$$\begin{array}{r} 95 \\ -32 \\ \hline \end{array}$$

$$60 + 30 = \underline{}$$

$$\begin{array}{r} 39 \\ +20 \\ \hline \end{array}$$

© Silver Burdett Ginn Inc. All rights reserved.

Name_____

Add or subtract.
Count on or count back.

1.
$$\begin{array}{r} 30 \\ +20 \\ \hline \end{array} \qquad \begin{array}{r} 51 \\ +20 \\ \hline \end{array} \qquad \begin{array}{r} 77 \\ +10 \\ \hline \end{array} \qquad \begin{array}{r} 96 \\ +\ 1 \\ \hline \end{array} \qquad \begin{array}{r} 66 \\ +\ 3 \\ \hline \end{array} \qquad \begin{array}{r} 23 \\ +30 \\ \hline \end{array}$$

2.
$$\begin{array}{r} 50 \\ -20 \\ \hline \end{array} \qquad \begin{array}{r} 37 \\ -\ 1 \\ \hline \end{array} \qquad \begin{array}{r} 74 \\ -30 \\ \hline \end{array} \qquad \begin{array}{r} 56 \\ -\ 3 \\ \hline \end{array} \qquad \begin{array}{r} 36 \\ -10 \\ \hline \end{array} \qquad \begin{array}{r} 59 \\ -\ 2 \\ \hline \end{array}$$

Find each sum or difference.

3.

Tens	Ones
2	4
+ 1	5

4.

Tens	Ones
5	8
− 3	3

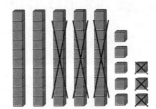

Solve.

5. A squirrel gets 3 acorns on Monday.
   On Tuesday it gets 6 acorns.
   On Wednesday it gets 9 acorns.

   The pattern is to add _____ more acorns each day.

6. Liz has 78¢.
   She buys a game for 51¢.   _____ ¢
   How much money does she have now?   _____ ¢

Name_____ **Performance Assessment**

What You Need

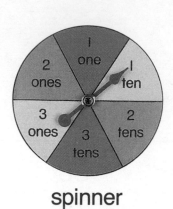
spinner

① Spin the spinner. Record.
  Add or subtract.

② Write the number sentence. Solve.

		Add or Subtract	Number Sentence
1.	46 +	1 ten	46 ⊕ 10 = 56
2.	68 −		___ ◯ ___ = ___
3.	34 +		___ ◯ ___ = ___
4.	57 −		___ ◯ ___ = ___
5.	45 +		___ ◯ ___ = ___
6.	86 −		___ ◯ ___ = ___

For Your Portfolio
You might put this page in your portfolio.

© Silver Burdett Ginn Inc. All rights reserved.

Circle the answer that makes sense.
Tell why.

1. Bill has 22 baseball cards.
He has 30 football cards.
About how many cards
does he have in all?

   about 10 cards

   (about 50 cards)

   about 100 cards

2. Cora has 69 shells.
She gives 20 to a friend.
About how many shells
does she have now?

   about 20 shells

   about 10 shells

   about 50 shells

3. Doug has 40 marbles.
He wins 17 marbles.
About how many marbles
does he have now?

   about 60 marbles

   about 10 marbles

   about 40 marbles

4. Patty plants 11 seeds.
Then she plants 32 seeds.
About how many seeds
does she plant?

   about 10 seeds

   about 40 seeds

   about 100 seeds

5. Chris has 49 rocks.
He gives 18 rocks to Kelly.
About how many rocks
does he have now?

   about 30 rocks

   about 70 rocks

   about 100 rocks

Name_____

Use a to add or subtract.
Write the keys you used.
Write the sum or difference.

Remember to press
 before you
begin each exercise.

1. 36+12

2. 56−24

3. 78−40

4. 39+50

5. 42+27

© Silver Burdett Ginn Inc. All rights reserved.

Fill in the ⬭ for the correct answer.

What are the missing numbers?

1. ___, 7, 8

⬭   ⬭   ⬤   ⬭
9   5   6   4

2. 42, ___, 44

⬤   ⬭   ⬭   ⬭
43 41 53 45

Add or subtract.

3.
```
  5
+ 2
```
⬭ 6
⬭ 8
⬭ 9
⬤ 7

4.
```
 11
- 8
```
⬭ 5
⬭ 3
⬭ 4
⬤ 2

5.
```
  8
+ 7
```
⬤ 15
⬭ 14
⬭ 16
⬭ 17

6.
```
  7
+ 9
```
⬭ 13
⬭ 14
⬤ 16
⬭ 17

7.
```
  8
- 5
```
⬭ 2
⬭ 4
⬭ 5
⬭ 3

8.
```
 13
- 7
```
⬭ 6
⬭ 7
⬭ 9
⬭ 5

9.
```
  8
  5
+ 5
```
⬭ 13
⬭ 10
⬭ 18
⬭ 17

10.
```
 26
- 2
```
⬭ 28
⬭ 21
⬭ 22
⬭ 24

11.
```
 30
+40
```
⬭ 70
⬭ 60
⬭ 80
⬭ 10

---

12. How much money is there?

⬭ 56¢
⬭ 43¢
⬭ 42¢
⬭ 52¢

13. Which one can you buy?

 40¢   27¢    31¢

○   ⊘   ○

---

14. How many equal parts are there?

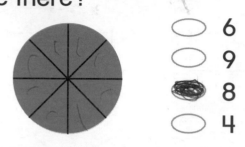

○ 6
○ 9
⊘ 8
○ 4

15. What part is orange?

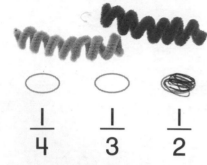

○   ○   ⊘

$\dfrac{1}{4}$ $\dfrac{1}{3}$ $\dfrac{1}{2}$

---

16. How many are there?

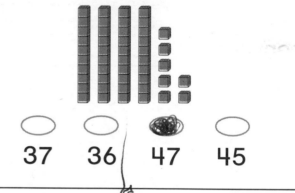

○   ○   ⊘   ○
37   36   47   45

17. What time is it?

⊘ 2:30
○ 6:00
○ 2:00
○ 3:30

---

18. Does this weigh **more** or **less** than 1 pound?

○ less
⊘ more

19. About how long is this?

○ about 1 inch
⊘ about 5 inches
○ about 10 inches

---

20. Choose the correct number sentence.

14 deer eat.
6 run away.
How many are there now?

○ $6 + 8 = 14$
○ $14 - 8 = 6$
⊘ $14 - 6 = 8$
○ $10 - 6 = 4$

Chapter 12 Cumulative Review

© Silver Burdett Ginn Inc. All rights reserved.

Name_____

add

2 + 3 = 5

addition sentence

4 + 2 = 6

after

7, 8

8 is after 7.

altogether

3   and   1

4 altogether

before

5, 6

5 is before 6.

between

6, 7, 8

7 is between 6 and 8.

calendar

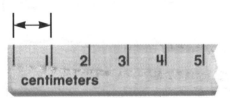

June						
S	**M**	**T**	**W**	**T**	**F**	**S**
			1	2	3	4
5	6	7	8	9	10	11
12	13	14	15	16	17	18
19	20	21	22	23	24	25
26	27	28	29	30		

centimeter

centimeters

circle

closed figure

Picture Glossary

cone

cup

corner

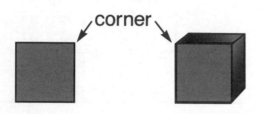

curves

count back

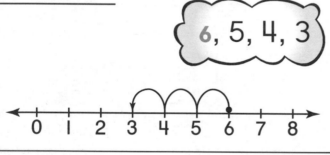
6, 5, 4, 3

0 1 2 3 4 5 6 7 8

cylinder

count on

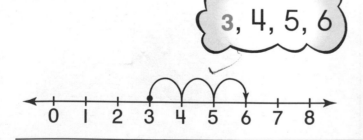
3, 4, 5, 6

0 1 2 3 4 5 6 7 8

decimeter

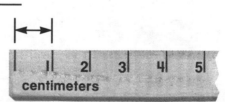
centimeters

10 centimeters = 1 decimeter

cube

difference

5 − 2 = 3

$$\begin{array}{r} 5 \\ -\ 2 \\ \hline 3 \end{array}$$

difference

© Silver Burdett Ginn Inc. All rights reserved.

Name_____ **Picture Glossary**

dime

 or

10¢   10 cents

fact family

$4 + 2 = 6$ $6 - 2 = 4$

$2 + 4 = 6$ $6 - 4 = 2$

double

$2 + 2 = 4$

fewer

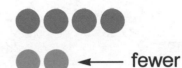

⟵ fewer

equal parts

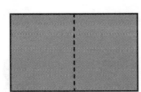

2 equal parts

foot

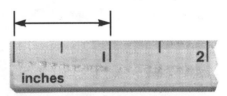

inches

12 inches $= 1$ foot

equals

↓

$3 + 2 = 5$

graph

Favorite Foods

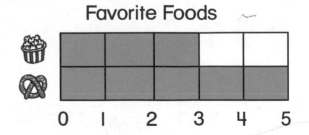

0   1   2   3   4   5

face

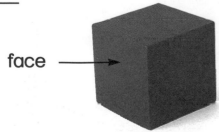

face ⟶

greater

4 is greater than 2.

Picture Glossary

<u>heavier</u>

heavier →

<u>kilogram</u>

5 peaches weigh about 1 kilogram.

<u>hour</u>

It takes about an hour.

<u>left</u>

5 minus 2

3 left

<u>hour hand</u>

hour hand →

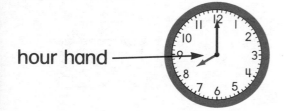

<u>less</u>

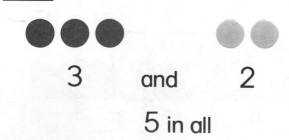

2 is less than 4.

<u>in all</u>

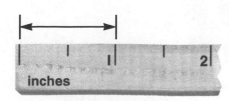

3   and   2

5 in all

<u>lighter</u>

← lighter

<u>inch</u>

inches

<u>liter</u>

© Silver Burdett Ginn Inc. All rights reserved.

longer

← longer

nickel

 or

5¢   5 cents

minus

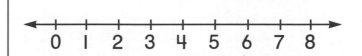

$$9 \underset{\uparrow}{-} 7 = 2$$

minus

number line

0 1 2 3 4 5 6 7 8

minute

I can count to 60.

It takes about a minute.

o'clock

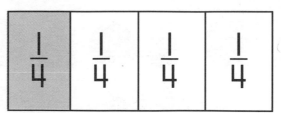

9 o'clock

minute hand

minute hand →

one fourth

$\frac{1}{4}$ $\frac{1}{4}$ $\frac{1}{4}$ $\frac{1}{4}$

more

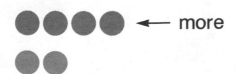 ← more

one half

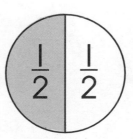

$\frac{1}{2}$ $\frac{1}{2}$

Picture Glossary

<u>ones</u>	<u>pint</u>
▪ ▪ ▪ ▪ 4 ones	
<u>one third</u>	<u>plus</u>
	$5 + 4 = 9$ ↑ plus
<u>open figure</u>	<u>pound</u>
	 3 apples weigh about 1 pound.
<u>pattern</u>	<u>quart</u>

<u>penny</u>	<u>quarter</u>
or 1¢ 1 cent	 or  25¢ 25 cents

© Silver Burdett Ginn Inc. All rights reserved.

rectangle

shorter

← shorter

rectangular prism

sides

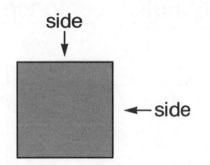

side

←side

regroup

 =

10 ones = 1 ten

skip count

2   4   6   8

related facts

4 + 3 = 7

7 − 3 = 4

sphere

same

same number

square

Picture Glossary

subtract

$$4 - 3 = 1$$

taller

taller →

subtraction sentence

$$7 - 3 = 4$$

tally

sum

$$4 + 4 = 8$$

$$\begin{array}{r} 4 \\ + 4 \\ \hline 8 \end{array}$$

sum

tens

2 tens

take away

3 take away 1

triangle

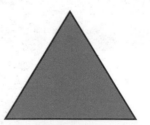

© Silver Burdett Ginn Inc. All rights reserved.

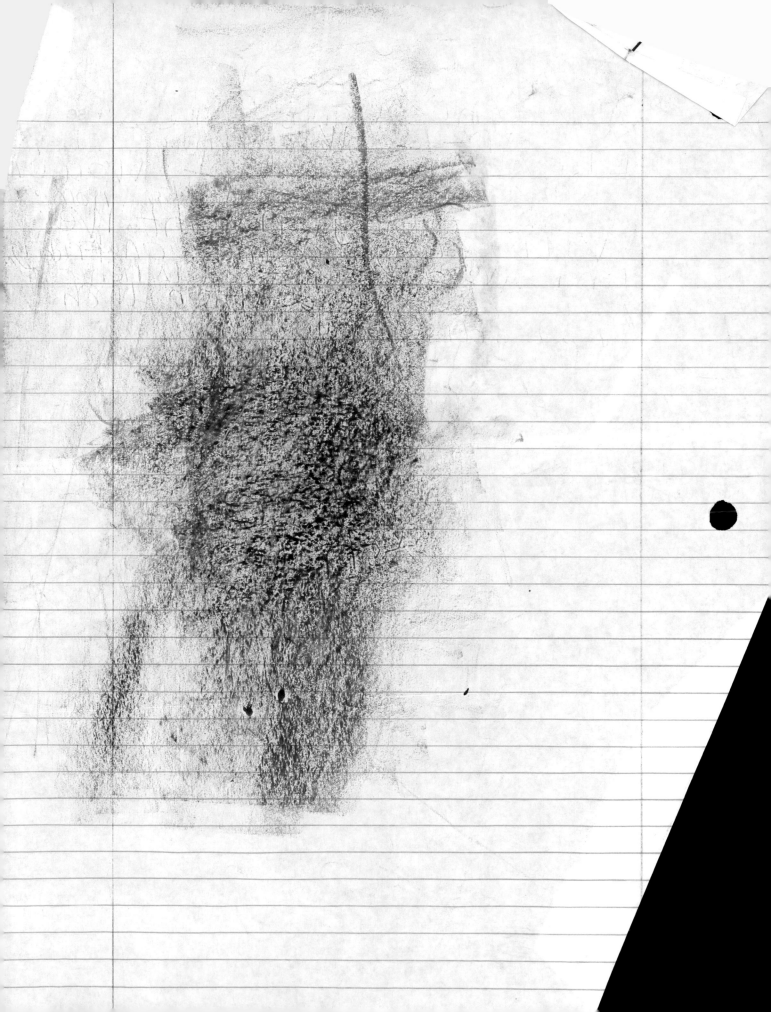

Name_____

1	one	
2	two	
3	three	
4	four	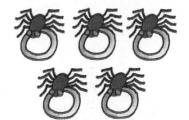
5	five	
6	six	

© Silver Burdett Ginn Inc. All rights reserved.

7	seven	
8	eight	
9	nine	
10	ten	
$\frac{1}{2}$	$\frac{1}{3}$	$\frac{1}{4}$

© Silver Burdett Ginn Inc. All rights reserved.

square	circle	cube
rectangle	sphere	cone
triangle	cylinder	rectangular prism

© Silver Burdett Ginn Inc. All rights reserved.

Dr. Rappoport 3-15
waiting 1hr
Very aggressive + not listening as a parent.
more movement.